FEUDAL ORDER

FEUDAL ORDER

A STUDY OF THE ORIGINS AND
DEVELOPMENT OF ENGLISH
FEUDAL SOCIETY

BY

MARION GIBBS

College Paperbacks

HENRY SCHUMAN · NEW YORK

CONTENTS

ACKNOWLEDGEMENTS

THIS book is largely a revision of some essays on English feudal society which were written during 1941—2, with help and encouragement from Mr. Christopher Hill, Mr. Rodney Hilton and Mr. Edward Miller. The revision was done during 1946—7 for the Past and Present Series. Conclusions and suggestions are of course neither final nor complete. If they provide a basis for discussion and further study, they will have served their purpose.

CHAPTER I

INTRODUCTORY

FOR several centuries after the fifth-century settlement of Germanic peoples, in parts of Britain and other former Roman provinces in Europe, a distinctive process of historical development took place. This brought into being a social order and civilisation which is worth study for its own sake and because it has played a major part in shaping the history of modern Europe. The object of this book is to outline this process of growth as it happened in England so that its place in history can be understood in a preliminary way by non-specialist readers. Perhaps the limitations of treatment imposed by this purpose can best be described by an analogy. A traveller who proposes to visit an unknown country does well to consult a map—a concentrated statement of elementary detail which will help him to find his way about intelligently and discover for himself the rich variety of the country and the people. An old map however decorative is of little use; neither is a map which shows only the chief towns, not rivers and mountains, roads and railways. Maps made for technicians are, as yet, outside his purpose or comprehension. Similarly in setting up landmarks for the preliminary study of a past historical epoch, the intelligent reader needs a concentrated synthesis of elementary detail and some general impressions which will indicate the many-sided character of the historical process in question and provide material for thinking, or beginning to think, about how and why it occurred and what relation it had to past and future epochs. A conventional little out-of-date summary of political history is of no use; learned monographs and articles are best read after the bare essentials of the subject and some of the primary problems which it raises, have been indicated.

The first, rather tiresome problem is the use of the word

feudal; can it be used to characterise the social order which
is the subject matter of this book? In current historical literature there are three usages of the term, each of which can
be defended, if not equally well. In the first place there is
the long established technical usage which arises from the
legal meaning of the Latin term *feudum*,* usually translated
into English as fee; this was the benefice or endowment of
land which a man of free status received from his lord for
his homage and service, usually military service. After the
Norman Conquest of England in 1066 the legal customs and
military system which arose from such grants of fees were of
great political importance for at least two centuries, and
English academic historians today usually insist that the
adjective feudal should be used only with reference to the
social relationships and obligations formed by the tenure of
fees. No fees, no feudalism, such is their dogma. In the second
place, as we have implied, the word feudal has been applied
to the whole social order which developed after the Germanic
Conquests in Europe, and so to all the principal features
of this society, including the relationships between manorial
lords and dependent unfree peasants, and the relationships
between lords and freeholders, whether they owned land
in their own right or held fees. This very general usage was
prevalent in the nineteenth century. In the third place,
feudalism is sometimes identified with the economic system
which prevailed in Europe before the rise of capitalism, in
particular with serfdom. Marxists have given more point to

---

* For the early history of the word see M. Bloch, *La societé féodale, la
formation des liens de dépendence*, pp. 254-260 (1939). He suggests that
the early forms behind the French word *fief*, were derived from a
word for cattle borrowed from the Germanic invaders: *vieh*. Until
the tenth century this loan word retained much of its old meaning,
but it was also used in seignorial households for the gifts of goods or
land which a lord gave to his vassals. *Feos* or *feus* was thus often a
colloquial equivalent of the Latin *beneficium*. Finally, Latinized as
feudum, it largely superseded this word in the age of mature
feudalism. If this is the history of an etymologically obscure word, it
epitomizes the character of the transition to feudalism and does not
justify a rigid use of the modern term, *feudalism*.

this usage, very common among economic historians, by linking it to their conception of epochs of historical development, each characterised by the evolution of a particular mode of production, which conditioned, as they suggest, the general character of the corresponding social and political process.* Feudal society, they will remind us, was a class society.

It is hoped that this minor problem of terminology will be incidentally clarified in the pages which follow. If it is necessary to use the term feudal only in its legal sense, italics will be used. As a matter of course, the word has often been used in a non-legal sense; for the Marxist conception of feudalism as an epoch of development in which the mode of production is fundamental, is a useful approach to the period following the Germanic migrations of the fifth century, in so far as it leads to matter of fact analysis of the changing structure of society. It would, of course, be absurd to confuse or ignore the distinction between unfree peasant tenures and free *feudal* tenures of land; from one point of view, a fee was an estate which gave its holder the right to live on the labour of the peasants settled on it. Nor should the word feudal usurp the place of the word manorial. In this preliminary study of the historical circumstances in which the disintegrating tribalism of the English peoples was re-ordered into a distinctive class-divided civilisation, the original need for the fee, knight service and the manorial economy which they presupposed, will be indicated; and then the rapid modification of these institutions as the economic process created new problems and new possibilities. For feudalism, regarded as a process of social development, involved the transformation of certain tribal institutions, the destruction of others. In close contact with surviving institutions of the Roman Empire, the leaders of the Germanic communities in western and central Europe became Christians and lords of estates. Sooner or later the peasants

* M. Dobb: *Studies in the development of Capitalism*, pp. 35-7.

under their dominion were depressed, producing a social order based on an expanding agriculture and commerce, in which landlords appropriated, either directly or indirectly, the surplus produce of their peasant tenants, and a small ring of landed magnates controlled both the military forces of the territories which they ruled and the Church. In the heyday of feudalism internal social development was constantly stimulated by economic and cultural contacts with Greek and Moslem territories in the Mediterranean and by extension of colonisation and conquest into Slav and Celtic territories, to the east and west of the original complex of Germanized territories, of which the English kingdom formed a unit.

Feudalism in its general, non-legal sense, was a term first applied to the "old order" in France before the revolution of 1789. So it became almost a synonym for what was thought of by the rising middle classes as reactionary and obstructive; the antithesis of the enlightenment. The eighteenth century tendency was to regard the whole medieval or post-classical period of European history up to the Renaissance of classical learning in the fifteenth century with contempt; to ignore or disparage its art and to dismiss its learning and religion as pedantry and superstition. For Gibbon it was a long night of Gothic barbarism. As subsequent historical research discovered the middle ages, these views were gradually modified. Before 1900, Maitland, one of the most critical and constructive of the great pioneer historians of the feudal social and legal system, could quietly suggest that feudalism was not unprogressive: *

"Feudalism is and always will be an inexact term . . . If we use it as we often do in a very wide sense, if we describe several centuries as feudal, then feudalism will appear as a natural and necessary stage in our history . . . The barbarian conquests being given us as an unalterable fact, feudalism means civilization, the separation of

* Maitland, *Domesday Book and Beyond*, p. 223.

employments, the division of labour, the possibility of national defence, the possibility of art and science, literature and learned leisure: the cathedral, the scriptorium, the library are as truly the work of feudalism as the baronial castle. When therefore we speak of the subjection of the peasantry to seignorial justice—we shall be speaking not of abnormal forces, not of disease, but in the main of normal and healthy growth."

No competent historian would now describe the process of feudal development as retrogression. Since Gibbon wrote his *Decline and fall of the Roman Empire,* indeed, since Maitland wrote the passage just quoted, archaeologists and historians have shown how bankrupt the Roman system was on the eve of the Germanic conquests of Western Europe. The creative contribution of feudalism to the development of civilization is slowly being realized by students of art, religion, literature, law, institutions. A revealing preliminary line of approach would also be through a study of development of the techniques of production and transport in the period, a very neglected field of research.* Primitive in comparison with the techniques of our own time they were superior to much of the practice of the Ancient World, where, until the late Roman period, the wide-spread use of slaves as manual workers held up technical advances. The reinforcement of human by mechanical energy, even in simple forms, enabled the productivity of labour to increase. Let us illustrate this point briefly; in subsequent chapters we can place some of the innovations more clearly into their historical context.

To begin with, there was widespread use of improved agricultural tools which made possible the cultivation of vast tracts of heavy forested land which hitherto had resisted all colonizing efforts. Population concentrated in these fertile reclaimed areas; the more primitive methods of stockraising

* Useful bibliographical references in L. White, *Technology and Invention in the Middle Ages,* Speculum, Vol. 15 (1940).

and cultivation were abandoned and experience gradually accumulated, by manorial bailiffs and gentry and richer peasants, which was finally concentrated and applied in the early stages of the agricultural revolution which ushered in capitalism. Meanwhile corngrinding, hitherto laborious manual work, was performed more efficiently and quickly by mills, wheels driven by the power of water or wind. And three simple devices enabled men to exploit more fully than in the Ancient World the labour power of horses: the nailed horseshoe which prevented broken hoofs; the rigid horse-collar made to rest on the shoulders of the animal to carry the traces (the Romans harnessed horses with flexible straps, one round the neck over the windpipe, so that the heavier the load the nearer the horse came to strangulation); and the tandem harness which made possible the use of a team of horses. Feudalism was the age of horse-power, on the battle-field and finally in production. For gradually, in the fields and on the roads, horses supplemented then began largely to supersede human porters and oxen. A network of routes connected together the numerous marketing centres of thirteenth century England to facilitate the collection of goods for overseas and coastal transport. This was cheapened by the building of heavier, wider better-rigged ships mainly dependent on their sails, not on oarsmen. Finally, towards the end of the thirteenth century the steering oar was re-placed by a fixed rudder, again a revolutionary invention, for in the long run it enabled larger ships, rigged with three masts, to be manoeuvred through heavy seas. From at least the twelfth century mariners often used a simple compass.

Meanwhile the watermill was being utilized in the expanding woollen industry, for fulling cloth. The crank was widely applied, for example in hauling up stone in building operations. An improved blast furnace made possible the casting of iron. And there were other minor inventions in the later middle ages: the wheelbarrow, which halved the number of workmen needed for short-distance carrying operations; the spinning-wheel, which speeded up the cloth industry; spectacles, which were a step forward towards the telescope; weight-driven clocks. These all seem humble advances, but cumulatively they help to explain why feud- alism finally produced an age of geographical and scientific discovery. Gunpowder and printing were not the only tech- nological inventions which ushered in capitalism.

Techniques form only one aspect of a mode of production. Before we attempt to analyse the origins of feudalism within a disintegrating tribal society, it may be helpful to outline generally some of the more obvious characteristics of feud- alism at the mature stage of its development. The fund- amental social cleavage in England, as on the continent, was formed by the exploitation of peasants by landlords. A section of these landlords were soldiers, another section priests; with sword and cross they protected the people, or so it was said to justify their privileged position in society. Small-scale production of foodstuffs by peasants for their own families was carried on alongside their forced labour or wage labour on the big demesne farms of landlords; and the economic initiative of prosperous peasants and landlords in increasing production for the market, made possible the regular exchange of goods and the emergence of specialised crafts to supply luxury commodities. There was both local trade and long distance trade.

Commerce did not, however, unify the kingdom even in the heyday of feudal progress. The traditions of the scattered communities of which feudal England was compact, villages, hamlets, and small towns, were rooted in their own fields and valleys, the countryside on which they imposed a pattern in the doing of their daily work. So at the basis of society there was a localism far more intense than anything we find today. Class struggles, for example, were localised: the complex conflicts within the towns, the resistance of peasants to landlord order, a conflict now hidden, now open, but normally accepted as part of the natural order of things. The isolation of one group of peasants from another, indeed the whole manorial system which kept the peasantry in their place, was the result of the primitive technique of production which in fact made impossible the support of large town populations, the knitting together of all the villages of England in the same economic ties. Towns developed slowly; each group of burgesses solved their local problems on their own initiative and in their own time. Even in 1377 not much more than eight per cent. of the population were townsmen, and only a minority of these had independent dealings with continental markets. Much of the overseas trade was in the hands of foreign mercantile firms; the bulk of the produce exported was wool and foodstuffs until the fourteenth century when undyed cloth became one of the chief commodities sold overseas. Feudal England was a part of feudal Europe, if economically a relatively backward part; she contributed to as well as received from the common cultural tradition.

Over against the divided peasantry and the townsmen with their petty local interests and outlook, stood the greater land-lords, the barons, prelates and the king. They were an organized political group, conscious of the community of their class interests. Below them the subordinate rural gentry gradually consolidated their position. They, with the barons and prelates, assisted the king in building up a central state machine whose powers, when effective, could reach out to remote villages and penetrate the liberties of the strongest of the barons. What it could not prevent was the petty tyranny of local agents. Hostility to them, and the machinery of oppression which they manipulated, is one of the domin-ant themes of later popular literature. Meanwhile the magnates looked beyond England for wider territorial domination: to the Celtic lands to the north-west, to France, to Germany and even to Italy. Their interests and culture were European; an English baron of the thirteenth century had more in common with a member of his own class in France or Germany than with the peasantry on his estate. Especially was the king European in his outlook and interests; after 1066 there were few kings of England who had not large dominions in France.

8

Idealizing and sanctioning the relationships of this divided society, more closely integrating it to the other feudal kingdoms of Christendom, was the power of organized religion—the catholicism of the Roman Church. Its mystifying conception of justice cloaked all social contradictions and gave colour to all social activities. The Church itself as a land holding institution was an inseparable part of the economic, social, and political structure of feudal society.

Feudalism flourished in a pre-scientific age. When the war lords of pre-feudal Europe first adopted Christianity they were at the stage when they could only express their attitude to society in poetic myths and rituals. They needed to learn many practical techniques and to develop what we would now call an educational system and philosophy of life if they were to advance from the barbarism of their background. At a later stage the dogmas of creeds, the collective chants and ritual of the liturgy, the perfectly concrete symbols of ecclesiastical art, the cycles of popular religious drama, and public sermons, formed the educational background of peasants and townsmen, as well as of an élite. Paganism had been pushed into the background.

Catholic discipline, as defined and sanctioned by the law of the Church, the canon law, was created in the feudal period. So we need not be surprised that it was well adapted to the needs of a class divided society. Nothing more sharply differentiates feudalism from tribalism and the society of our own time. Now few religious teachers insist that man is a "living soul using a body" which must pass either into heaven or hell. In England no mass popular belief responds to the suggestion that life is a preparation for death and should be regarded as a very difficult journey which only ends well, in heaven as distinct from hell, if the unhappy traveller begs for divine assistance from his "patron" saints and the "holy Mother of God". There is no fear that by refusing baptism or other sacraments of the Church, a man condemns himself to live in a real hell ruled by the devil. The claim of priests to have a monopoly over the dispensation

of the "saving" sacraments and to interfere in every department and phase of our lives, are therefore taken very lightly.
It was different in the villages and towns of feudal England,
where superstition and illiteracy were as universal as poverty,
where the tithe-collecting monk-prelate might be hated but
not scorned, where the parish church and its ceremonial were
a necessary part of everyday life. The priests, of course taught
different social moralities to different classes: the rich man
could reach heaven by almsgiving and the poor man by
patience and hard work. It was these conflicting moralities,
including attitudes to money-lending, to relationships between master and servant, to work for God or Mammon
which protestants had to break down or modify before they
could function freely as capitalists.* We cannot understand
the feudal social order without understanding the part which
the church played in it; nor can we understand the Catholic
Church in modern Europe and the anti-clericalism which it
has aroused. To ignore, satirize, or whitewash the activities of
the medieval Church, or to forget that its system was in fact
built up by successive generations of men, living in particular
historical circumstances, would be a major distortion of
history.

CHAPTER II

DISINTEGRATING TRIBALISM

HISTORIES of England usually begin with an account of the
peopling of the whole island of Britain by prehistoric
European tribes. This may lead to an initial error. England
was only part of Britain. The coming of the English to this
island marks a decisive cultural break in the history of
the lowland regions where they settled; and the subsequent

* R. H. Tawney, *Religion and the Rise of Capitalism* (1926).

history of these regions, rightly called England, was closely linked with the rise of civilization in Northern Europe whence the English had come. The channel and the North sea formed a highway, not a barrier. English contacts with Franks, Frisians, Danes, Normans and with Mediterranean culture, through merchants and missionaries and invading armies, were vital, while contacts with the fringe of British peoples to west and north were of very secondary importance. The background to the rise of feudalism in England, therefore, should be the European background. Important as European prehistory is, there is no need to go much further back than those large-scale population movements of the Germanic peoples, which marked the final collapse of Roman hegemony in Western Europe. For they created the situation which determined the lines of the feudal epoch of cultural development. To indicate how and why they took place is therefore our first problem.

This means a glance at the late Roman Empire. For long before the Germanic conquests of the fifth century the Western provinces were in a state of economic decline and political crisis. The Germanic peoples pushed their settlements beyond the imperial frontiers and established their kingdoms on Roman soil precisely because the Roman attempt to bring Celtic and German lands into the orbit of Mediterranean civilization had failed and ruined peoples at whose expense the experiment had been made. Obviously it is important to understand this, otherwise the Germanic conquests would appear catastrophic and the whole process of feudal development a retrogression.

Romanization in the provinces of Gaul and Britain and in the Rhineland had at first proceeded with superficial rapidity. City life was artificially fostered at convenient and widely scattered centres; for the city, so the Romans believed, was the means by which Roman rule could be accepted by one section of a conquered people and imposed upon the rest. Cities were not only military and administrative centres; business men from the more developed parts of the Empire set up workshops in some of them, imported slaves, engaged in trade, and bought up land to develop for commercial purposes. There the native aristocracy learnt to live like Romans and were drawn into the service of the Roman state. With their temples, market-places, public baths, and other sophisticated amenities the cities of both Gaul and Britain bore witness to the policy of grafting an exotic civilization on to a tribal society.

The attempt broke down. In fact the burdens of maintaining the Roman system far outweighed the advantages of the *pax Romana*. The city placed impossible burdens on the countryside; the rapacity of officials and soldiers in getting supplies for the city populations and the army, cut across the interests of business men. The army itself was increasingly recruited from the more barbarous populations over which the Romans ruled; to control it became politically more expedient than guarding the interests of civilians. Nor could industry develop so as to link up province with province while the mass of the people, peasantry, artisans, slaves, lived below the poverty line. Both transport and the technical equipment of industry were nearly as primitive as they had been in the days of the Greek city state. Slaves could revolt and peasants rebel, but only the army could effect a political revolution. The lawyers could proclaim the equality of man and emperors could introduce new laws, but this scarcely resolved the economic crisis. Inflation, depopulation, the steady contraction of trade, the ruin of all but the wealthiest citizens, the re-emergence of wide flung estates to which masses of poverty-stricken tenants were attached: such were the forces which were undermining town life and the policy of Romanization as early as the third century. In Britain the towns soon sank into decay, sometimes before their grandiose public buildings had been completed. Invading armies and pirate bands in the fourth century may have found slum populations squatting among the ruins. But after the invasions of the fifth century the cities were probably desolate and uninhabited, objects of romantic wonder to men who knew how to build only timber houses. "Wondrous is this wall stone . . . there courts are in decay and there lofty gates; the woodwork of the roofs is stripped of tiles; the place has sunk into ruins, levelled to the hills."*

The crisis of the third century was followed by the desperate and not entirely unsuccessful efforts at reconstruction on the part of the imperial government. Catastrophic military defeat was staved off until the fifth century. In Britain, the urban landowners, mostly the Romanized native nobility, retreated to their country estates or villas and lived there in semi-Roman comfort, protected by the imperial defence system from restless Celtic tribes and Saxon pirates. This small minority of the population of Britain was prosperous enough. (Only some five hundred villa sites have been discovered.) On some estates industry developed, mainly to supply local needs. But it is significant that the extension of the area of cultivated land into fertile forest areas came to an end. The poorer peasantry lived, as they had done before the Romans came, in upland villages;† here a primitive husbandry was maintained which was incapable of expansion; infanticide was practised. In short, the presence of Roman armies and governors in Britain impoverished and degraded the backward peasantry, it did not Romanize them. Probably all the conditions which led to serious peasant revolts in Gaul existed in Britain too. And the failure of the Romans in Britain to develop the productive resources of the countryside and to win the loyalty of the native peasantry was deep-rooted in their system. They did not lack the skill to convert forest into arable land. But the owners of villas who dominated the best of the open, well-drained land in the civil province, had no incentive to extend their cultiva-

* *Anglo-Saxon Poetry* (ed. E. K. Gordon), p. 92.

† R. G. Collingwood and J. N. L. Myres, *Roman Britain and the English Settlements*, pp. 221-5. This also discusses the significance of depopulation on the Wiltshire Downs, and development of the Fenland, which occurred towards the end of the Roman period.

tion; by so doing they would only have increased their share of taxation. And the native peasantry had neither the skill nor the resources, nor perhaps the freedom to become pioneers. Many must have been tied to big estates, as *coloni*. Increasingly the state concentrated on defence of the frontiers, relying more and more on the manpower of Germany for its army recruits.

In Britain the inroads of primitive barbarians were disastrous. From the great raid of A.D. 369, when Picts and Scots had acted in collusion with Saxon and Frankish pirates, there was no real security within Britain. As the legions were gradually withdrawn to the continent—for to maintain a remote outpost of Empire like Britain was less important than defending Gaul and Italy—the villas became the primary objects of barbarian attack. They were burnt or looted by invaders from all sides, or at least evacuated, before the English began to settle in the province in considerable numbers (after 450). The British princes who organized resistance to the English invasions, among them the legendary but still historical Arthur, were all but barbarians in the eyes of Rome. Their power was based in western Britain, which had scarcely been Romanized. They were defending not the Roman system but a Celtic-Christian civilization which was developing in isolation from Roman influences radiating from Gaul and Italy.

On the continent the breakdown of Roman life was never so complete as in Britain. Completely derelict towns and deserted Roman estates characterized Britain only. In Gaul and to some extent in the Rhineland, the Frankish immigrants settled among landowners with a veneer of Roman-Christian civilization, in regions where attenuated Roman towns still functioned as administrative, ecclesiastical, and even commercial centres. They had no desire to destroy these survivals of the past. On the contrary, the civilization of the Empire, barbarized, impoverished and decadent though it was, excited their admiration. It was, so to speak, their long-familiar inheritance. The Franks were rapidly converted to Roman Christianity, and the upstart barbarian kings, Franks or Goths, desired nothing more than recognition from the Roman Emperors who continued to rule over the Eastern provinces of the Empire from Constantinople. Even after the Arabs had overrun Africa, Spain, Syria (in the seventh century) and occupied Sicily, the Emperors in Constantinople dominated the Eastern Mediterranean. The development of the barbarian kingdoms in England, Germany, and the northern regions of Gaul was deeply influenced by this survival in parts of Europe of a barbarized Roman-Christian civilization, and by the survival of the Byzantine Empire.

Who were the English peoples, from whom did they come, what was the level of their culture on the eve of their migrations? The home of the Angles and Saxons in the fourth century A.D. lay in the heart of Ancient Germany, in the region between the Eider and the Weser. But the Saxons, as we shall see, pressed hard upon the Frisians and the Franks; and the *English,* as the Germanic settlers in Britain can collectively be called, were drawn from all these northern European peoples.

What Tacitus wrote about Germany at the end of the first century A.D. is useful and relevant, if it is interpreted critically.* There is also Cæsar's earlier account, and other fragments of evidence bearing on North Germany, literary and archæological. Even so, we know very little. We can be certain, however, that from the second century our English ancestors, like other Germanic peoples, severally were forming increasingly formidable military federations. But their progress in the arts of peace, east of the frontier provinces, could scarcely have been considerable. Conditions favoured war and plunder. Tacitus had described peoples who had assimilated an Iron Age culture: that is, they utilized metals, including iron, for tools and war

* See the edition of the *Germania* by J. G. C. Anderson, 1938; also R. Koebner's remarks in *Cambridge Economic History, I,* pp. 13-18.

weapons; they grew corn but not in great quantities; they herded cattle. Cattle, indeed, were their chief form of wealth. They rejoiced in the number of their herds. This phrase, considered together with other features of their tribalism, helps us to realize that in Tacitus' time cattle-lifting, plundering raids and the seizure of settled land seemed easier to these peasant warriors than the development of forested and waterlogged land near at hand. Germany, Tacitus reported, was shaggy with forest and marsh. Agriculture was practised only on relatively open, well-drained soils; fields were quickly made and easily abandoned. Although the heavy plough was used for tillage, only a small part of the available land was turned into arable; and this tilled land was shifted annually to another part of the common land (common in the sense that a group of families used it for their pasture and arable). The untilled land was used for pasture. The tillage lay in a compact block; for by this arrangement less labour was required both for ploughing and setting temporary fences round the growing corn. Shares in it were allotted according to rank. So, at least, Tacitus said. This primitive 'extensive' type of agriculture was one of the causes of the aggressive restlessness of the Germanic peoples east of the Rhineland, of their perpetual land hunger. For, given this farming technique, increasing population soon outran subsistence. Unable or unwilling to clear heavily timbered land, some of the tribesmen in northern Germany made settlements along the crumbling coastline, on artificially raised hillocks rising from the marshy flats and relied mainly upon fishing and herding for food. "When the waters cover everything around they are like sailors on board ship; when the sea retires they pursue the fish receding with the tide. . . . They dig peat up with their hands and dry it more in the wind than the sun. And yet these tribes, were they to be conquered by the Romans, would call it slavery."* Pliny the Elder was here writing contemptuously of the

---

* Quoted by Hodgkin, in *History of the Anglo-Saxons*, I, p. 368.

Chauci; but many of the Frisians and Saxons were living in much the same conditions on the eve of the folk migrations. On the other hand, tribesmen filtrating into the Rhineland and Gaul came into contact with Roman agriculture and commerce. We cannot assume that all the various immigrant peoples who collectively can be called English, had reached the same cultural level.

Expansion into new lands, or the more intensive development of land already in their power: such were the alternatives facing the peoples beyond the Rhineland. Conditions, as we have said, favoured the former. Tribesmen with access to the sea gradually acquired more skill in shipbuilding and seafaring. Piracy became the chief occupation of adventurous spirits. From the third century 'Saxon' ships carried bands of warriors westwards along the coast to Frisia or Gaul, and thence to the shores of Britain. The villas and towns of weakening provinces lay open to attack, acting like a magnet on the prolific starvelings from the rude and inhospitable north. These 'Saxon' raids, so we can infer from traditions later incorporated into Old English poetry, were led by lords, self-constituted leaders, who could steer a ship through stormy waters, fight with courage, and treat their boon companions with generosity. Such war bands were one of the features of disintegrating tribalism. Successful leaders took their place among the nobility and gloried in their heroic deeds and military prowess. Minstrels celebrated their adventures and feuds in epic verse. The cult of Woden, religion of warriors, was developed at the expense of fertility rites, although the latter survived among the peasants. The surplus wealth of society, the proceeds of plundering raids, concentrated in the hands of war lords. And plunder could be combined with trade, loot exchanged for war weapons. For several generations raids proceeded; the first isolated ventures being followed up by the formation of permanent pirate bases west of the Rhine. Angles, Frisians and Franks seem to have been drawn into the confederacies of 'Saxon' war chiefs. And when, in the second half of the fifth century, after the Franks had occupied Gaul and the Lower Rhineland, a massed attack was made by the 'Saxons' in the South East of Britain, Franks and other peoples shared in the enterprise. The main Anglian migrations, however, proceeded independently; the river valleys to the north of the Thames, draining the eastern plain of Britain, were thinly peopled by Anglians by the end of the fifth century.

The English established their early settlements in face of determined resistance from the British; and, in the interior, this resistance continued for more than a century. During most of the sixth century the English were secure only in regions in the east and south-east of Britain. The wide tracts of forest which the British under Roman rule had scarcely begun to clear, kept groups of the invaders in isolation. Fen and forest, for example, separated the Anglians of the Trent Valley from those of the Humber estuary. The South Saxons were unable to link up with the men of Kent because of the impenetrable woodland of the weald. The Middle Angles were cut off from the Severn Valley by the forest of Arden. Within the regions which they had appropriated the invaders sooner or later settled down to farming, applying their own farming methods, even when their land lay where Roman villas had existed. It is noticeable that they did not take over the upland villages of the backward British peasantry. It is indeed extremely difficult to discover how far this peasantry survived under English rule. Districts vary one from another in this as in other matters. There is no coherent history of the English people during this dark age of transition; only the unrecorded struggle for survival of scattered tribal groups, clinging precariously to their settlements, achieving in the course of four or five generations a more stable organization adapted to local conditions.

The darkness created by lack of evidence hides momentous changes. When the obscurity begins to lighten, that is, when written evidence can again be used to reconstruct social conditions, the English settlers were on the threshold of a new age. In thought and desire and in the words of their min-

strels, the descendants of noble families and even the rank
and file of the tribesmen, might live in an age of plunder,
piracy and land-grabbing, but the heroic age had in reality
passed away. Conditions of chronic instability no longer
prevailed. Opportunities for plunder were constantly
diminishing. As the boundaries of the English dominions
were extended into the interior and reached the highland
regions, tribal expansion ended, warfare between increasingly territorialized kingdoms took its place. The victories
of the English over the British in the later sixth and early
seventh centuries were the prelude to the age of colonization,
in which peasant communities struck deep roots into the
soil throughout the lowland regions, and extended the area
of settlement within the lands under their control by
economic initiative.

On the eve of this movement the English were still tribal
peoples organized for war, not unlike Greek society as de-
picted in Greek heroic verse. England was still an undeveloped country in which vast tracts of woodland were more
conspicuous than ploughland and pasture. But the scattered
settlements were organized within kingdoms, or rather
within the organic units of the kingdoms (*provincia* or
regio, or, to use Germanic terms, *mægth, gau, lathe, scir*.)
These were not so much territories as communities of tribesmen who felt themselves bound together by common customs
and blood-ties; sometimes one or two hundred families, sometimes considerably more. The small kingdom of Kent, for
example, was compact of eleven regions; the farmsteads of
each family in the community were dispersed over the
countryside; to each was attached a ploughland of about two
hundred acres; collectively they enjoyed pasture rights over
stretches of undivided forest and marshland adjacent to
their region. Each holding contributed to a communal food
rent levied for the support of the king. Tribesmen also owed
occasional services at the king's *tun* which formed the
regional centre. Here, under the presidency of a royal reeve, a
monthly open air court assembled to transact common busi-

ness and to settle disputes. Here the people were responsible both for declaring custom and executing their own decisions. Their decisions, in so far as they were only an application of custom, were binding on everyone and unanimous. Co-operation in the maintenance of personal rights merged imperceptibly into co-operation in maintaining the community's obligations to the king. These included military obligations; the tribesmen were either active warriors, or a reserve of fighting men. In kingdoms other than Kent, although the basic type of agricultural settlement was sometimes different, very often village settlements,* the community of the *regio* found a means of collective action in a court which acted as the link between them and the king.

We have spoken of families. Almost certainly we should think of a patriarchal family as typical, rather than the small two generation family of our own age.† Each would live, with or without slaves and dependents, in the same homestead, to which was allotted a share of land (in many English districts called the *hide*, or, in the equivalent Latin phrase, *terra unius familiæ*). In a tribal society with a low level of material culture the cell of social life is the *kindred*: marriage customs, the education of children, the initiation of adolescents into the adult life of the tribe, economic activity, defence, the taboos, customs and ritual which regulate these, usually

---

* See below, p. 44.

† M. Bloch in *Cambridge Economic History, I,* pp. 268-9. On the whole it seems improbable that all or even most of the early English settlements were made by such families: see F. M. Stenton, *Anglo-Saxon England,* p. 314 note, on the dubious evidence of place names ending with *ingas*. On the other hand, given the background of tribal custom, patriarchal families would form within two or three generations, from which sooner or later, some members would depart, to form new stocks, or to become dependents of lords. The survival of partible inheritance into the later middle ages, in Kent and some districts of East Anglia, for example, presuppose joint families. For this practice and later practices of impartible inheritance, see Homans, *English Villagers in the Thirteenth Century.* Yardlands, created by lords for tenants from whom labour services were exacted, were not subject to division between sons; they were divided only at the will of the lord.

rest on the kindred. But when economic life has advanced far enough to enable an *inheritable* surplus of wealth to accumulate in the hands of kindreds, the disintegration of the kindred into patriarchal families sets in. This creates the need for more complex social organization. Now what we have said about the families and folks of seventh-century England carries with it the implication that the primitive kindred group was no longer predominant in either economic or social life. The family of two, three or four generations, the agricultural settlement, and the regional community were the groups in which the individual tribesman lived his life. But a kin group wider than the family could act on occasions. There were still rules determining the degree of affinity within which marriage could take place, rules of inheritance within the family group and when direct heirs failed. A man without kindred, or a man cast out by his kin, was without rights, an outlaw, unless he was adopted by another kindred, or found a lord to vouch for him. Social discipline was still maintained largely by the kin, so that a man or woman might be involved in the misdeeds of their kin-group. For example, if a man of another kindred was killed, the whole kindred of the killer was responsible either for paying *wergild* or blood money to the kin of the murdered man, or, if this compensation were refused, for sustaining the blood feud. When a tribesman was accused of an offence, he could clear himself by the oath of a given number of his kindred swearing to his innocence. (A man's circle of kindred included both maternal and paternal relatives). But homicides within a kindred group occurred frequently, a sign of its disintegration and growing ineffectiveness. The practice of a man *seeking lordship* increasingly provided an alternative social discipline. For a good lord gave his man the material support which a father gave his sons, and the social protection which the kindred gave its members.

Equality of social status as between man and man did not exist; even in Ancient Germany social distinctions had existed. In the first place some tribesmen possessed slaves, although we do not know how many. The slave was as much a chattel as an ox. He could be acquired in war, or purchased, or slavery was legally imposed as a penalty. He could be beaten, put in bonds, or sold. He had no rights in the tribal courts, no claim on tribal lands. Slaves, however, were usually allotted a hut and an acre or more of land; this tended to transform their status into that of a poor and dependent peasantry. Then there was a half free class: either freedmen or British communities who had accepted English rule. Finally, freemen were divided into two groups: the ceorls, the typical tribesmen, the peasant warriors of the *folk*, owning land inherited from their families, and the legally privileged freemen or nobility. The latter were mostly warriors ennobled by their service to kings, gesiths or thegns. Like some of their ancestors, the war lords who organized the migrations, they formed a self-conscious élite of warriors. Each might be surrounded by a following of young warriors. On their loyalty, military prowess and companionship, kings depended both in peace and war. Their higher social standing was sanctioned by a higher wergild. And there is little doubt that the lands given by kings to nobles, as rewards for the services of their youth, made their estates more extensive than the family lands of the ordinary freemen. Even as reeves of royal estates, and it is probable that they sometimes served the king in this capacity, they stood above the rank and file of the tribesmen.

And what of the kings and their kingdoms? Kings, as we have implied, were commanders-in-chief; they drew food rents and services from the folk regions;* they had royal lands within them, the king's tuns. This was an embryonic political system and as such significant. Royalty, moreover, was inherent in a particular kindred. The kings of the various seventh-century kingdoms all claimed descent from Woden. But what conviction was evoked by this claim? What potency

---

* Land assessed for such public services was later called folkland in contradistinction to privileged land or land held by book or charter: see below, p. 40, and F. M. Stenton, *op. cit.*, pp. 306-9.

was attached to such magical rites as a king may have performed? What was his relationship with the heathen priesthood?

It is hard to say. New problems of a practical kind were
emerging in the seventh century. Could kings exact fines
from wrongdoers? Did the powers of kingship extend to clari-
fying custom, or sanctioning innovations like, for example,
the introduction of Christianity? What rights did they exercise over unsettled land within their dominions? What control could they exercise over the gesiths and thegns who
formed their military entourage and who owed them the
loyalty and service due to a lord? They regarded him not
only as a goldgiver and breadgiver but the giver of land.
How could a king who was not conquering new lands reward
his men without impoverishing himself or the tribal communities of his people? How could he *compel* obedience?
The feudal relationship between lord and man—tenure of
land on condition of service—was as yet undreamed of.
Kings and nobles, on the whole, still looked outside their
own people for plunder. The heroics of war had more interest for them than estate management.

The personal, precarious character of kingly power was
fully realised by the poet who produced *Beowulf,* the most
important epic poem surviving from the Old English period.
The eloquent alliterative verse of the epics, the art of professional minstrels, had its roots far back in the heathen
past, and although it had become closely associated with the
kingly and noble classes, minstrels used forms and material
long familiar to the people; both language and content concentrated the experience of several generations in clear symbols. They sang of the exploits of the heroes of the migrations, colouring old themes with the problems and tensions
of their own time. Through the skill with which they did
this they had the power to shape social sentiment. Thus in
the idealized picture of the Danish king's court in *Beowulf,*
there was conscious archaism tinged with hopelessness and
regret. All this had passed away. Beowulf, in youth the hero

of the age of plunder and adventure, became in maturity the unfortunate king of the period after the migrations who must command the loyalty of self-seeking followers or fail in his duty of strengthening and defending his people. In his last fight Beowulf was deserted by his followers, all but one who proclaimed imminent disaster: "Now is there prospect of a time of strife for the peoples when the fall of the king becomes widely known to Franks and Frisians".* Loyalty to a lord was the supreme virtue, betrayal the supreme shame; but betrayal was inevitable.

This was in the last quarter of the seventh century. In the eighth century the sense of an attractive age which had come to an end was stronger:

"Kings and givers of gold were not as they once were when they wrought among themselves deeds of glory and lived in lordly splendour. This host has all fallen. The delights have departed. Weaklings live on and possess the land, enjoy it by their toil."†

At the opening of the seventh century the English kings, at least in the south-eastern kingdoms, commanded considerable wealth, considerable, that is, compared with the bare level of subsistence at which most of the ordinary tribesmen lived. There was limited but peaceful trading between their countries and the Franks and Frisians. For example, the tomb recently excavated at Sutton Hoo in East Anglia contained magnificent treasure, evidently acquired by trade, as well as by plunder. Ethelbert, king of Kent, ruled over a kingdom where town life was re-emerging at Canterbury and Rochester; he had secured some hold over the city of London, that port of call for continental traders, and exercised overlordship over all the kingdoms and peoples south of the Humber. The territories dominated by the East Angles, by the South Saxons, by the Middle and East Saxons, were small

* *Anglo-Saxon Poetry*, p. 64.

† *Ibid.*, pp. 84-6, contains a translation of *The Seafarer*, the poem from which this passage is taken.

but more or less well defined kingdoms by the opening of the seventh century. The Mercian and West Saxon kingdoms were consolidated more slowly because of the undeveloped character of the interior of Britain, and the difficulty of establishing a frontier against the hostile Welsh. Beyond the Humber were Anglian groups of peoples, interspersed with a considerable number of Britons. Generally speaking, then, seventh-century England was a *heptarchy* of kingdoms. Kentish supremacy was succeeded by East Anglian, East Anglian by Northumbrian; then the Mercian kings, tentatively in the last decades of the seventh century, more confidently in the eighth century, basing their power on the Midland regions which they now controlled and London, achieved an overlordship over England south of the Humber more solid and permanent than that which Ethelbert had exercised. Not until the ninth century did the dynasty of the West Saxon kings gain the ascendancy.

It may seem a far cry from tribalism to feudalism, but only if rigid formulations of these words are cherished. The society which we have described in bare outline was a society in transition, in which tribal traditions were still strong; but it possessed excrescences which, given certain stimuli, could develop at the expense of the older tribalism and become part of a new social order. In fact there was more transformation than destruction. For example, the superiority of the king over the folk region was exercised so that the latter became an administrative division of a kingdom dominated by landlords not the rank and file of the tribesmen. The practice of kinless men seeking lords, the enslavement of freemen, lordship over free military companions or vassals, were some elements out of which the feudal social order was built up. In the early seventh century, however, such development was only potential; there was as yet very little to differentiate the English from the Germanic communities in other parts of Europe where Roman influence was negligible. The external conditions for progressive advance lay partly in the fact that the English had occupied a land where there was ample space for expansion—fertile land hidden under trees and undergrowth; and partly in the fact that in the seventh century they were coming into contact, through the Franks and the Roman Church, with more sophisticated traditions than their own.

CHAPTER III

CONVERSION TO CHRISTIANITY

ENGLISH contact with the Roman tradition* came mainly through the Roman Church. For there was no Romanised population within England, no survival of Roman institutions. In this England was like Germany east of the Rhine, unlike the Frankish dominions in Northern France. Before their migrations the English had only indirectly been influenced by the Empire. Thereafter, as we have implied, there was some limited intercourse with the Franks. When, however, the kings and nobility of the English kingdoms were duly baptised and became the patrons of Roman priests, interaction between the Germanic and Roman traditions was sharp and potent. Possibly kings acted to save their souls; even so, they could scarcely have been blind to the far-reaching decisive implications of their conversion. In fact they grafted onto the life of the peoples they ruled a mature religion, a foreign literature and language, an organisation with a highly sophisticated political tradition behind it, which had power to set in motion changes which could transform their tribal life.

The most remarkable characteristic of the Roman Church, even in the early stages of its growth, was its power to assimi-

---

* It should be remembered that this was by no means an exclusively Western tradition.

late new influences and to adapt itself to changing circumstances. Its continuity was secured by a series of reorienta-
tions which, each in its own way, increased the church's
religious appeal and administrative strength. The early
obscure persecuted Christian brotherhoods, which existed in
the greater cities of the Empire's eastern provinces were influenced by the mystical philosophies, the Stoicism, the popular mystery cults, which they challenged. In this highly
sophisticated environment, without discarding the teaching
of the apostolic age, they created a theology, enriched their
ritual, and modified their organisation until the bishops of
local churches and the priests and deacons whom they ordained, emerged as a distinct order, concentrating all
spiritual authority in its hands. They were still however men
of no great social standing. The next transformation came
after the year A.D. 312, when the Emperor Constantine gave
toleration to this irrepressible, many-sided religion, which
was spreading rapidly throughout the Empire. It became the
state religion. The Emperor became its defender. Bishops
were endowed with large estates. In the decaying cities of the
western provinces, fast slipping out of imperial control, the
bishops became the most important of Roman officials. Yet
they were, so the Pope or Bishop of Rome claimed, subject
not to the Emperor but to St. Peter (who was said to have
been the first bishop of Rome). To the Pope in particular, as
to St. Peter, belonged the keys of heaven and hell. "Render
unto Caesar the things that are Caesar's, and unto God the
things that are God's." The traditional words of the founder
of the Church became portentous in this age, when the things
that belonged to God came to include wide tracts of land,
and the distinction between clergy and laity was more
important than that between Christian and pagan.

In the parts of Britain which the English occupied,
organised Christianity disappeared during the storms of successive invasions. In the continental provinces of the Western
Empire the church not only survived but the bishops increased their local influence; in particular the economic and

civil power of the Pope in Rome and in the regions of Italy where papal estates lay was strengthened. The Church in Italy was not yet cut off from the Church in the Eastern provinces of the Roman Empire. While the barbarians allowed the Church to go on existing, the Church undertook the task of converting and educating them. Thus it consolidated its position, began to expand into new territory, and to react to barbarian influences. The conversion of Clovis, the king of the Franks, by far the most important of the barbarian leaders, was its first signal victory (A.D. 496).

In the new European situation created by the Germanic invasions of the western provinces of the Empire, the Church's economic role became important. "Living supporters of the Roman tradition of estate ownership and estate management," churchmen applied this knowledge to the practical problem of making their expanding estates more productive. (Roman landowners accepted ecclesiastical offices and transferred their estates to churches in many cases.)* They began to play a part in the work of clearing the derelict land or the many wooded and thinly settled regions which they controlled, and transmitted this art to their Germanic neighbours. In the disturbed period of transition they stood for order, good management, stability, confidence in the future, and this in the circumstances was a progressive factor. The part which they played in the colonization of England we will consider in the next chapter, along with other aspects of the economic movement of the period.

The continuity of the Church at this time also necessitated the preservation of the cultural legacy of the ancient world. In the West this was a barbarized legacy, but rhetoric and law, poetry and music, natural science and philosophy, the arts of making records and writing history, architectural techniques and various decorative crafts—all this was, by the fifth century, more or less intimately connected with the

* R. Koebner, in *Cambridge Economic History, I,* p. 43.

Church's life. St. Augustine of Hippo, the great African bishop, in A.D. 410 started that great critique of pagan philosophy and justification of the Church, the *City of God*. His theological writings, constantly reiterating the dependence of man on the grace of God, became the text books of the Middle Ages. Early in the sixth century a new form of religious community came into being, admirably adapted to the task of transmitting both religion and civilizing arts to the heathen districts. This was the monastery as organised by St. Benedict in Southern Italy. It was monks trained in this Benedictine tradition who were sent by Gregory the Great, "most imperially minded of all the Popes," to England. Indeed it was the great churchmen of this catastrophic age, St. Augustine, St. Benedict, and Gregory the Great, who shaped the essential characteristics of that militant feudal Catholicism with its emphatic emphasis on the need for an organised sacrament-dispensing priesthood, which was to develop during the Middle Ages in such a spectacular way.

Before turning to the effects of conversion to Roman Christianity on English society, one further point may be made. The Germanic war lords of Europe allowed the Church to go on existing and eventually became its converts because it was useful to them. Faced with the problem of consolidating and developing kingly power they sooner or later turned to churchmen who would place their learning and knowledge of affairs at their disposal. The political experience of the Roman world, however, was taken over by the barbarians very gradually, with free adaptation. It was absorbed within their own traditions. Even more obviously the cultural legacy of Rome was only slowly and partially assimilated. So closely identified with the Church was this gradual inter-penetration of Germanic and Roman traditions, so original was the civilisation that was its outcome, that, when feudalism was in decline, the anti-clerical intellectuals of the rising middle classes were able to rediscover a "dead" antiquity and to find in the style and facade of "classical" literature the antithesis of the styles which they despised. They little realised that it was precisely through the development of feudal-Christian culture that a "Renaissance" was possible. It is important not to perpetuate their error; the Renaissance was mainly the continuation by a new class, for new purposes, of the intellectual activity of the Middle Ages.

II

Looking back through the Middle Ages to the year A.D. 597 it is easy to colour the arrival in that year of Roman missionaries at the court of Ethelbert, king of Kent, with an epoch-making significance. To do so is to exaggerate. This mission was only the prelude to the mission of 668 from which the effective work of the Roman church in England as a whole dates. Nevertheless we can be certain that Bede's story of the origin of the Roman mission was intentionally superficial. Pope Gregory, so he said, on ascertaining that the angelic-faced slaves in the Roman market-place came from England, made a series of Latin puns and resolved to snatch the souls of so fair a people from hell-fire.

What were the facts which bear upon the situation? Britain from the papal point of view was a former Roman province in which Christianity and the iniquitous heresy of Pelagius had flourished. The English formed a heathen wedge between the Franks, who were converts of Rome, and the Welsh and Irish who were Christians who had lost contact with Rome during the fifth century. Ethelbert was the most powerful of the rulers of the English, as we have noted. He was moreover a dependent of the Frankish ruling house. One of their women was his wife and practised her religion at his court. Pope Gregory could select Ethelbert's court from among all the other heathen courts of Europe, for three reasons. First, the conversion of England might please the Frankish rulers whom Gregory was anxious to work with in reforming the Church; secondly, he intended it to lead to the establishment of bishoprics throughout Britain; thirdly, and perhaps this was the dominating consideration, this would be a step towards bringing the Celtic church into subordination to the Roman See. Certainly Augustine's orders were to establish contact with the Welsh bishops and secure their obedience and co-operation in the task of converting the English. But Wales was in communication with Ireland, and Irish monks from their colony of Iona, off the West coast of Scotland, were at this time starting to evangelise not only the peoples of Northern Britain, but the decadent Christians of Western Europe. They were ascetics and men of learning, as heroic and enterprising in their missionary activity as in an earlier age heathen war bands had been in the search for land and plunder. Already Columbanus' work among the Franks and the Burgundians of the continent had brought home to Gregory the possibility of Celtic enthusiasm drawing all the churches north of the Alps away from their allegiance to Rome.

St. Augustine and his mission had little permanent success outside Kent. On the whole, the English did not take kindly to these strange priests from Italy who despised their heathen rites and tribal customs, who demanded not only hospitality but gifts of lands, and who had been sponsored by the formidable Franks who, in Europe, had been subjecting other Germanic peoples to their rule. Heathendom was strong in England as it was in Germany. Moreover, to strengthen their position in Northern Britain, and to gain British support against the aggressive Mercians, the Northumbrian king Oswald summoned monk-missionaries from Iona to his court (A.D. 634). These monks converted the Northumbrians and won over some of the Midland peoples. It should be noted that in Wales, in Ireland, and in Scotland Christianity was being organised on a tribal-monastic basis. Celtic Christianity had no sophisticated political tradition behind it

So for a generation the two rival Christian organisations competed for influence in England. Spontaneous intercourse with Europe was meanwhile intensified. The chief centre of the conflict was in Northumbria. A section of the Northumbrian court, led by the able, ambitious prelate Wilfred, a Northumbrian noble who had studied Roman clerical organisation on the continent, forced a decision in favour of the Roman Church. This was at the Synod of Whitby (664). The Irish monks returned to Iona. Wilfred was given a bishopric; Rome was informed of the new developments. Thanks to the opportune death at Rome of the Northumbrian king's nominee for the archbishopric of Canterbury, the Pope was able to send to England two ecclesiastics of great distinction to organize a diocesan system in England and to introduce Roman customs in cathedrals and monasteries (A.D. 668). One was an aged, learned Syrian monk, Theodore of Tarsus, a refugee in Italy from the insurgent Arabs, now archbishop of Canterbury; another was a younger monk and refugee from Africa, Hadrian; he had exchanged his abbacy in Italy for that at Canterbury. Both men proved able to apply experience gained in the long Christianized Mediterranean countries to the problems of England. Through them and native pioneers like Wilfred and Benedict Biscop, who like Wilfred was a Northumbrian noble who travelled through Europe visiting various ecclesiastical centres including Rome, hundreds of Englishmen learnt to look to Rome for leadership. Organized in monastic or semi-monastic communities they were caught up into the movement for establishing the Roman Church in England on a permanent basis.

Let us first look at this conversion through the eyes of Bede, an Englishman trained at the monastery of Jarrow, founded by Benedict Biscop. His best known historical work, that remarkable piece of scholarly propaganda significantly called the *Ecclesiastical History of the English People* (A.D. 732), is evidence of the ideas and policy of the clergy who had been most active in promoting change and organization on Roman lines. For, as Bede tells us, he wrote his history in collaboration with them. He selected and dramatized his incidents, or added documents from the papal archives, which were copied for him by a London priest, with a conscious effort to put across an official as distinct from a personal view of the conversions in England. These he presented as the triumphant conquest of ineffective heathen magic by all-powerful true religion, made possible by a succession of providential accidents and saintly acts. The conflicts which accompanied it were understressed or entirely glossed over. For example, Bede, in describing the way in which the Northumbrian royal circle was first converted by Paulinus of the Gregorian mission, told at length how the pagan high priest of the Northumbrians expressed doubt of the potency of his own rites and spells to win battles and to advance his own interests, before he himself violated the pagan sanctuaries; a noble less cynically reflected that paganism gave no understanding of the problem of why life passed into death, did nothing to lighten the dark mystery of beginning and ending. Were these attitudes as typical as Bede wanted us to believe? Thinking into facts incidentally used by Bede for his own purposes, we can be certain that there were usually diplomatic motives at work in the acceptance or rejection of baptism; opposition came from many quarters, including some pagan priests and some royal and noble families who, perhaps, were half suspicious that their whole privileged position, their chances of success in battle were endangered by the preaching of those powerful strangers competing with them for influence over the king and his bounty. In A.D. 616, for example, the sons of the converted East Saxon king, Sabert, in defiance of their father's memory, drove Bishop Mellitus from their territories; in the same year the Londoners, perhaps led by their high priests, refused to allow the same bishop to enter their city. Redwald, king of the East Anglians, erected a temple in which there was an altar to Christ and an altar for sacrifices to pagan gods. Another East Saxon king, a priest-ridden convert, was killed by two members of his kindred because he forgave his enemies instead of fighting them (the negation of the blood feud, a deeply rooted convention of tribal society). Many of the kings who took refuge in Christian monasteries shortly after 664 may have done so to escape the furious tensions of their courts.

The conflict between Irish and Roman monks within the kingdoms, according to Bede, turned on various technical points: for example the date of Easter, the shape of the clerical tonsure. For unity of the English Church could scarcely be built up by attacking the saintliness of monks who had lived very humbly and travelled up and down the wild countryside of the Northumbrian kingdom preaching to unimportant tribesmen. Moreover by Bede's time the Irish Church had accepted the Roman customs on the disputed points; polemic was unnecessary. Nor was it tactful to emphasize the issue which Wilfred had apparently made clear at Whitby; the English must not be tied down to two remote islands on the edge of the world, inhabited mostly by wretched Celts, when they had the opportunity to enter the rich orbit of Roman civilization, where prelates lived like princes. And why did Bede so fiercely attack the British heretics* of the fifth century? Was he indirectly attacking contemporary Welsh Christians or was it merely deference to Augustine's authority? Or was opposition to the claims of priests being created by their advance? Or was there on the part of Bede and his friends, some theoretical understanding that Augustine's emotional mysticism furthered clerical interests, while the heresy developed an attitude of mind that led to rationalistic criticism? Perhaps all considerations operated together. In any case Bede, like Gregory the Great, laid all possible emphasis on the spiritual power of the priests and bishops—the power to dispense sacraments and

---

* Followers of Pelagius who denied St. Augustine's view of 'grace' as a divine force which overwhelmed and used the individual human will. This view of 'grace' lies behind the emphasis on sacraments which on St. Augustine's authority influenced the moral teaching of the Catholic Church and gave wide powers to the priests as priests. Bede was also a bitter opponent of Arianism, the heresy which had infected the Germanic peoples coming from the Danubian regions.

the power to excommunicate. Compromise on matters connected with priest-craft was inconceivable.

Bede, however, could approve of the conversion of heathen temples to Christian worship; he took care to quote Gregory's letter: "If these temples are well built, it is clear that they ought to be converted from the worship of devils (i.e. heathen gods) to the service of the true God; so the people may the more familiarly resort to places to which they are accustomed." And as they kill many oxen in a sacrifice to devils, Gregory continued, some similar solemnity on some Christian feast day must take its place "for it is impossible to obliterate everything at once from obdurate minds." (Bk. 1. 30)

Fertility rites, it should be remembered, survived in various semi-disguised forms far into the feudal epoch. Belief in faith healing, in the power of God to strike down the unbeliever, in miracles which could be wrought through saints and their relics, (in short in the Christian magic which was based on, but formed a counterpoise to the old magic), should be fostered, as Bede took care to do in many chapters of his history. And missionaries could play upon primitive fears of death and belief in an after-life, by painting the terrors and tortures of hell and purgatory, and the contrasting bliss of heaven, insisting upon the value of repentance, implemented by gifts of land to a priest who would pray for and save their souls. The recording of visions of hell was very relevant to Bede's purpose.

In conformity with the policy of compromising with the elements of heathen tradition which were not considered dangerous, the church used the current popular art of poetry as a medium for education. Together with the sermon it was a means of reaching the unlettered. Of course the Church looked askance at purely pagan poems, but did not discourage their adaptation to Christian purposes. Members of monastic communities turned biblical stories and legends of saints and apostles into verse, in which many of the conventions and phrases of heathen epic poetry were utilised. They thus made the new heroes the focus of pre-existing sentiments. Indeed, poets and listeners accustomed to identify themselves with a Beowulf who overcame disturbers of the peace, the outcast evil monsters who haunted the waste, would find it easy enough to excite or be excited by the story of Satan's rebellion and fall into hell, or of Christ's harrowing of this place of torment. Christ crucified was a "young hero . . . firm and unflinching";* his cross, eloquent in the Roman world as an instrument of slave torture, became a military banner, a symbol of victory over evil. His apostles became a warband: "twelve glorious heroes . . . eager leaders and active in war, bold warriors".† The clerical life itself became a kind of warfare; as the monastic rule told the would-be monk, "he must take up the arms of obedience and fight under the banner of the Lord Christ, the true king".§ Facts of this kind have aroused rationalists to outbursts of anti-clerical ardour. It is not with this purpose that attention has been called to them. They, and still more the sources from which they were taken, explain the *process* of conversion. The existence of a mature, purposeful ecclesiastical policy, the persistence of heathen attitudes to life as the substratum of Christian worship and sentiment, hell fire presented as the punishment of iniquity (thieves and malefactors, false men and fornicators and the forsworn, were placed in hell by the author of a poem on Christ); by these varied means, tribal traditions were gradually weakened and communities of clergy established in the heathen kingdoms. These in their turn began to change the structure of society both by the acquisition of land and the application of the various arts practised in monasteries.

Let us illustrate this latter point by taking particular examples of monastic communities: the cathedral church at Canterbury which Hadrian reorganized; Benedict Biscop's

* *Anglo-Saxon Poetry*, p. 262.
† *Ibid.*, p. 200.
§ *Rule of St. Benedict*, Prologue

monastery at Wearmouth-Jarrow, founded in A.D. 674. Land for the support of the latter house was given by the North-umbrian king: the number of monks soon reached six hundred (an abnormally large number); all had to be clothed and fed. Corn of various kinds, fish, vegetables, honey, cheese, butter, eggs, wine, rather than quantities of meat, were the foods which were needed. Instead of the primitive wood or dry wall buildings which had satisfied the Celtic monks, Benedict Biscop brought stone-masons and other craftsmen from France to build a church in the Romanesque style with glazed windows. From the continent he also procured paintings which illustrated the life of Christ, embroidered robes and chalices for use in the church, and a library of books. Incense and wine were probably imported too for the altar service. In other words he gave his community a standard of living which made necessary a new attitude to agriculture and to monastic industry. Also to domestic management; for the daily routine of monastic life demanded the careful keeping of time hour by hour, week by week, year by year; and the methodical measuring out of all supplies of food and clothing. The use of a calendar and of Easter tables, of primitive instruments for telling the passing of the hours, of standardized weights and measures, and sooner or later the keeping of accounts, were the not un-important consequences.

The members of a monastic community under their abbot formed a brotherhood who shared in common resources at the discretion of the lord abbot. A very important constitu-tional difference marked it off from all other contemporary associations; for example from the war band of a lord. A monastic community lived under a written rule: the rule of St. Benedict in which so much Roman tradition was con-centrated and the use of which was now spreading beyond Italy. They discussed business in a general chapter with reference to this monastic code as well as to their own local traditions or customs. Their vows had a legal as well as a religious character: they included the vow of stability, life-long membership of the same community. Like slaves they had to serve: God being pictured as an all-seeing benevolent invisible master who would treat deserving monks like sons and give them a place in his heaven, while condemning the disobedient to torture and perpetual bondage. This idea was reinforced for the monks by the physical presence of their abbot: not only their *father* but their *lord*, allotting tasks to all; a master to be obeyed as if he were indeed an incarnate god.

What was called the monks' service was of three kinds: manual work, perhaps in the fields, gardens, cowsheds, or workshops of the monastery (and in Bede's time even a noble put his hand to the plough, the axe, or the smith's hammer); public prayer, which required knowledge of how to read Latin, how to chant in rhythm, and involved ritual which on the great feasts was sometimes incipient drama; and finally, literary study. Those willing to become scholars must have been in a minority; but the libraries of a monastery like Canterbury contained the texts and reference books necessary for learning to read and write in Latin, and for the study of the scriptures, church history, and theology. A little logic, law, medicine, natural science might incidentally be studied. The learning of Greek was fostered at Canterbury by Hadrian, but this was exceptional. The text-books used were mainly those current in the late Empire; in biblical study and theology, St. Augustine and St. Gregory were dominant authorities. All work was supposed to be accompanied by prayer and asceticism, and the end of all discipline was complete detachment from the physical world. Fortunately, this was too intensely theoretical an ideal to achieve, and most monks seem to have saved themselves from this kind of self-frustration by taking part in a community life which offered so many opportunities of human activity at a civilized level. In fact, the life of the community was arranged so that able monks could apply themselves according to their abilities to estate management, preaching and teaching, the copying and illuminating of manuscripts, the art of the liturgy, history-writing, and various other intellectual studies. Aldhelm at Canterbury, in apologizing to the bishop of Winchester for not keeping an appointment, pleaded that he was dealing with students, who "among other studies were exploring the decisions of Roman Law and the secrets of jurisprudence".*

Monks also became involved in affairs outside the monastery: as missionaries, advisors of kings, messengers to the Pope. Many went far afield. English churchmen during most of the eighth century dominated Northern Europe. They were in constant contact with the Papacy and the Franks. Bede's works were circulated on the continent as well as in England. Boniface and other English missionaries, supported by Popes and Carolingians, converted the Frisians and organized a church in Germany. Alcuin, a Northumbrian scholar, went to the court of Charlemagne to help carry out the educational and religious reforms which that most powerful of Frankish kings desired. English cultural leadership in eighth-century Europe illustrates excellently the decisive effect of their contact with Roman Christianity.

The practical problem of how to support and how to protect the clergy, which all the tribal kings had to face after 668, was solved by the clergy for them. What a prospective ruler of a diocese or monastery wanted was a gift of land, such as the kings gave to their followers. This the clergy represented as a gift to God and his saints, which would be a perpetual claim for prayers for the salvation of the donor's soul. A solemn record of the gift was made in a charter or land book. Disputes concerning land so given were not to be settled by the regional courts, but by the king and his leading men, who now included bishops as well as nobles. Heavy fines for infringing the church's land right were allowed and exacted. In addition it was sanctioned by an ecclesiastical blessing and curse—perpetual bondage in hell to those who violated its sacredness. So the Church helped

* M. R. James, *Two Ancient English Scholars* (Glasgow, 1931), pp. 13-14.

English military chiefs and kings to develop some notion of privileged property. And the clergy with their knowledge of barbarized Roman law, thought of land as property which could be leased or sold, or willed, outside family and kindred. Sales and bequests of lands to the Church by private persons, if confirmed by the king and his leading men, gave the Church the same kind of privileged property which they obtained by gifts from the king. Land right so acquired, sometimes rights to food rents and other services owed by the peasantry, sometimes rights over a more or less undeveloped stretch of property, became the basis for ecclesiastical lordships or estates, as we shall see in the next chapter.

The setting up of cathedral churches and the delimitation of the dioceses dependent on them was started by Theodore of Tarsus and more or less completed by the time of Bede's death (735).* At the same time bishops and kings were founding minsters to serve as regional centres from which the bishop's clergy could carry Christianity to the peasantry. Subsequently parishes were formed; usually through the action of the rising class of lay landlords. In villages which they dominated they made a plot of land available for a graveyard and a church building, and gave ploughacres for the support of a resident priest. They also nominated the parish priest and claimed to control all the revenues which the church attracted: plough alms, church scot and tithe. The latter was regarded as a voluntary payment in the time of Bede, and was not monopolised by the parish churches. But by the middle of the tenth century this heavy charge upon the land, a tenth of the produce of fields and flocks and herds, was enforced by law. For it was the landlord patron of the church who disposed of tithe, not the resident priest. Behind these proprietory rights over the churches was the background of tribal heathen custom. As we started

* Reorganisation was however necessary both after the Danish invasions of the ninth century and the Norman Conquest of the eleventh century.

by saying, the Germanic peoples in assimilating what the Roman world had to offer adapted it to their own traditions.*

Landlord exploitation of church revenues, royal control over bishops and their appointments, had not been envisaged by Bede. He had condemned in no uncertain terms the monasteries which had been created in Northumbria by lay landowners who wished to avoid both services to the state and the discipline of the Roman church. But in the age of conversion, as in many other periods of Church history, responsible abbots and bishops put ecclesiastical interests first, their loyalties to their benefactors second. The role of kings was to endow their churches and to protect them. In return prelates would use their influence in upholding royal authority in preserving peace, in acting as mediators in feuds and disputes. They would even give monarchs the title of kings "by the grace of God". In introducing the ritual of anointing kings churchmen reinforced, indeed transformed, the heathen notion that a king participated in the divine. It is noticeable that the kings who first issued codes of law for their subjects before Alfred's day were kings over whom Roman prelates had influence. On the other hand, so far as the bishops were concerned, any king who failed to give adequate protection to their churches, to repress disturbers of the peace, was unworthy of his office. Better that someone more effective should take his place. For the dynasties of the petty English kingdoms as such they had no respect. Their pretensions to descent from the sons of Woden deserved contempt. Accustomed as the bishops were to meeting together to deal with ecclesiastical business and passing decrees which were to be valid throughout England they tended to support the dynasty which, for the time being, was in the ascendant, and seemed likely to rule over all England.

* Ulrich Stutz, *The proprietary church as an element of medieval German ecclesiastical law* in G. Barraclough, *Medieval Germany*, II.

What we have written so far may suggest that the effects of conversion to Christianity, including the psychological effects worked themselves out at two levels: the economic and political. In England as in many other parts of Europe, the formation of ecclesiastical estates was part of a wider movement—the extension and improvement of agriculture and the subjection of the peasantry to the power of landlords. Ecclesiastical discipline and learning and institutions, ecclesiastical ideas about law and justice and the duties of a Christian king, enriched and modified political conceptions implicit in the tribal kingdoms. The unity of the Church, as it has often been said, preceded the unity of the state in England. It is time to turn to the broader aspects of the growth of landlordism and a landlord state, movements to which the conversion to Christianity had given so important an impetus.

CHAPTER IV

VILLAGE AGRICULTURE AND THE GROWTH OF MANORS

THE agricultural changes which paved the way for the rise of landlordism may have started in the period of settlement before the conversion of England. If so they are lost in the obscurity of a dark age. What is certain is that they were proceeding in the later seventh century. Records begin at this time, so it can be written of without the kind of speculation which led nineteenth century historians to project the village community of the Middle Ages back into ancient Germany. It was a period of comparative peace. The British areas in the interior of England had been conquered; the Welsh had been driven back into the highland regions; the English kings had accepted Christianity; Wessex and Mercia had consolidated the Midland peoples under their rule.

There was, then, relative political stability and some sense of security. Meanwhile, in the regions of the primary English settlement wealth had accumulated—cattle and slaves as well as treasure. Customary tribal experience of farming could now be supplemented by the knowledge of estate management which ecclesiastics who had been in contact with the continent might well possess. And, perhaps the decisive factor, increasing population acted as a stimulus from below for the extension of settlement into the areas of damp oak wood forest, while the pressure of kings or those to whom they had transferred their rights over folkland operated from above.

The more primitive of the English peoples must have brought with them into Britain the practice of extensive farming. From this, advance could be made by abandoning the wasteful practice of cropping now one tract of land now another, concentrating labour on the clearing and cultivation of permanent fields on fertile soils.* In the regions of Kent where the first settlements had been made in homesteads isolated from each other, each with their share of arable land, development could proceed by more systematic and intensive cultivation, so that holdings became mainly arable farms supporting only the animals required for field work. Swine, sheep, cows, were pastured in outlying forests and marshes which until the ninth century were the individed collective property of the men of the region. In many areas however, including areas of difficult settlement where damp oakwood forest was prevalent, the typical unit of economic life was the village; development of the surrounding land proceeded from nucleated groups of homesteads, and, at least in Midland villages, the holdings of the various families of the village were closely intermingled in the extending arable field. Through agricultural settlements of a village type, many thousand acres of the wolf-

* See reasons for abandoning extensive farming suggested by C. S. and C. S. Orwin, *The Open Fields*, pp. 38-9

haunted forest land, including some of the most fertile soil in England, were converted into corn-fields; meadows were formed along the alder-choked alluvial beds of rivers and streams; population concentrated in the river valleys. In Orwin's phrase men 'tamed the wild'; and this was an agricultural revolution of nameless peasants more important in human history than those which were carried out by capitalist farmers in the next epoch.

The tempo of this movement towards more and better agriculture, this colonizing movement which allowed population to expand, lifted the peasantry above the insecurity and poverty of tribal conditions and enabled lordship to emerge, was slow; development was uneven. The details of the process vary from region to region. We will consider it in the regions where open-field villages became typical. For here, most clearly, we can see that the movement was the achievement both of peasants who wished to stake a claim in particular parcels of land and of more powerful lords, discovering and practising the art of peasant exploitation. In writing of the lay-out of the open-field village Maitland surmised that such a 'wasteful, cumbrous, and barbarous plan' was made by tribesmen 'willing to sacrifice economy and efficiency at the shrine of equality'.* We wish to show, on the other hand, that it was the commonsense solution of problems produced by new circumstances, made by men who were learning how to assimilate new and more advanced methods into their long-established practice, and who, incidentally, were used to inequality in the allotment of land.

First, let us get a picture of the layout of the open-field village in the undulating river valley country of the midlands; it is easy to do so, at least for the period after the Norman Conquest when the system had crystallized, because there is fairly ample material. We should imagine a huddle of primitive farmsteads, perhaps ten, twenty, or more, lying

* Maitland, *Domesday Book and Beyond*, pp. 337-8.

along a 'street' on a site which provided shelter and water as well as easy access to the surrounding countryside. There would also be a sprinkling of huts where lived poor peasants owning neither ox nor horse; dominating all, the village church, and perhaps the barns and stables and dwelling-house of the lord of the manor, or if the village had more than one lord, a corresponding number of establishments which displayed some outward signs of lordly privilege and greater wealth. Around such a nucleus of buildings stretched the village lands—meadows, ploughlands, and pastures. The striking feature to us would be the absence of permanent enclosing hedges. The hay meadows bordering the banks of the stream were undivided. The ploughland stretched away as far as the eye could reach, broken only by 'sikes' of rough land across which the plough could not pass, and the grass trackways which gave the ploughteams access to the furlongs. These were blocks of *lands** ploughed to follow the slope of the ground so that water could drain away, divided from each other, as in a ploughed field to-day, by double furrows. The so-called fields were complexes of furlongs each subdivided into *lands;* in all they might be above a thousand acres in extent. Beyond these ploughlands were the unenclosed pastures merging into waste: fen, moor, or woodland. Here perhaps were a few isolated homesteads and here the village sheep and geese and cattle grazed. The woodland provided either acorns or beech masts for pigs, wood for fuel, building material and implements, berries, nuts, game, and so on. They were part of the commons so necessary for the whole community's livelihood.

Just as all the villagers grazed their cattle on the commons alongside beasts owned by the lord, so everybody's arable lay intermixed; the village farmers had their holdings scattered in acre or half-acre units across the fields. These open fields and undivided pastures made necessary a system of

* A technical term for what sometimes is called the strip. Lands were not divided by turf balks, as Vinogradoff thought: see C. S. and C. S. Orwin, *The Open Fields,* pp. 126-7.

production in which all the members of a village group co-operated in care of livestock and tillage. They were also, very often, the framework of a system in which a big majority of the peasant cultivators held their land on condition of working for a considerable part of their working time with their own oxen and horses, or with their hand tools, on the *lands* of the open fields whose crops were appropriated by the lord, the lord's demesne. The demesne could be very large, perhaps as much as half the total acreage of the fields; the typical holding of a tenant farmer or villein was a thirty acre virgate, or borate, or half virgate, or some other standard unit; the holdings of the poorest class were very small, five acres or under. For landlords had acquired hereditary rights to exploit their peasants, to develop customs by which they stood to gain, and to obtain such control of the village resources as they could in practice maintain.

Here, then, interlocked in the village were the contradictory features of co-operative peasant production and landlord control—features characteristic not only of English midland villages, but of similar settlements throughout Europe, where too they were widespread but not universal.

"When the Homeric chieftain counts his possessions, he enumerates his household goods, his slaves, and his livestock, but he does not mention the pastures on which his cattle graze, and it is at least doubtful whether he regards even the land he cultivates as his own."*

If we substitute English free tribesman for Homeric chieftain the statement would stand for early seventh-century England. It would not however be true of the England described by the Domesday Survey made in 1086. Then the peasant knew where his acres lay, and so did the lord. The lord moreover often claimed that specific common rights of pasture and rights to clear the waste were permitted by his good will for a specific rent in cash or kind; uncultivated

---

* G. Thomson, *Aeschylus and Athens*, p. 37.

land was landlord land. How had such claims come into being? Why beneath them did co-operation persist?

It is logical to consider first the plough, for it was the plough in action which shaped the pattern of the open fields. What kind of plough was in use? This is far from certain. Not the primitive scratch plough or *aratrum,* used, for example, in the British upland villages; on heavy clay soils this was a useless implement. Perhaps not the heavy wheeled plough which some of the ancient Germans were said to have used and which may have been introduced into England by the Belgae and used on the villas of the Roman period. Orwin has demonstrated convincingly that the plough used for making the raised ridges and double furrows of the *lands* of the open fields need have been equipped only with a mould board, an iron coulter knife and ploughshare. He therefore postulates the existence of an early form of the swing plough used in the midlands up to the nineteenth century. His argument deserves consideration. In any case a team of eight oxen was normally required for heavy ploughing. Wherever then the lie of the land permitted, long furrows were ploughed, thus reducing to a minimum the time taken in turning the plough. The furrow length was never so long that a *land* could not be completed in a day's work. The area ploughed in a day lay behind the standard land measure, the acre.

These *lands* were in effect cultivated co-operatively; only the crops were individually owned in any absolute sense of the word. For ploughing, peasants had to pool their oxen to make up a team of eight oxen*; for the maintenance of idle oxen in the conditions of scarcity which then prevailed was not a practical alternative. To understand the urgent

---

* Seebohm suggested that strips were allotted in rotation, as ploughed, to those who brought their oxen to make up a common team; hence from co-aration, an old tribal practice, arose the system of holding land in scattered strips. See F. Seebohm, *English Village Community,* pp. 113-14. Co-aration was certainly the basis of field divisions in Wales; *op. cit.,* p. 120. See also Orwin, *op. cit.,* p. 41.

need for co-operation between peasant families we have to keep in mind the constant fear of famine, the low level of subsistence, and conditions in which the village population was expanding both by the natural increase of families and the admission of strangers. Hence the need for establishing new homesteads in the village and extending existing arable fields into the waste; or alternatively, for the formation of a new settlement. Clearing, tillage, and the care of livestock : each activity involved a diversity of tasks and heavy labour. Division of labour and continued co-operation were neces- sary. In this pioneer period there was so much to do that only essential work would be undertaken by the village community. For example, if the holdings of villagers were intermingled in common fields, less labour was required to fence growing crops from the trespasses of cattle than if holdings were isolated from each other. Again, labour time was saved if the common arable fields were ploughed sys- tematically furlong by furlong. More than this, the common fields facilitated the rough planning and supervision of the various operations of ploughing, sowing, and harvesting, whether by a village reeve or the reeve of a lord. The scat- tering of individual holdings over the furlongs arose natur- ally: from co-aration or from piecemeal clearing or by division of holdings between children; but it made easier the use of common plough teams and indeed, the main- tenance of co-operation throughout the farming year. It distributed, if it did not equalize, shares of good and bad land, of land near and far away from the village. The risk of the whole of a peasant crop being destroyed by some unfor- seen mischance was reduced to a minimum. In short it was a solution of various practical problems, rather than an archaic method preserved out of a passion for equality. Tribal custom was in the background, becoming progres- sively less important as the new system was worked out.

In villages where the economy was dominated by a religious house or other lord, the open-field system was as convenient as when the villagers were free peasants owing services only to the king. In the time of Ine of Wessex a king consciously used his position to maintain land in cultivation and to enforce the communal obligations of villagers. (About A.D. 694.)

"If ceorls (i.e. free peasants) have a common enclosed pasture or other land to hedge about and some have hedged their part and others not, and their beasts graze on the common cornland or grass, let those responsible for the gap go and give to the others who have hedged their part the compensation that is awarded."*

In the larger villages, at least, co-operation required local organization; hence the need for a village court. In villages dominated by landlords with big demesnes, these courts eventually passed under landlord control, and became manorial courts.

A technique of better tillage, at what seasons to plough, how deep to plough, and so on, was worked out gradually. This was linked with the maintenance of the fertility of the arable, the fundamental agricultural problem. Here as in other fields of activity Germanic tribesmen learnt from a Roman practice, adapted it to their needs, and began to improve on it. For fallowing was a Roman practice; it became an essential part of the open field system. The two-field rotation was first adopted: half the acreage of arable was alternately sown with corn while the other half was fallowed. Wasteful of land as this was, the system was considerably more productive than extensive farming. In the two-field rotation half the corn land was sown with winter corn, half with spring corn, and the fallow field was turned over by the plough twice or, later, three times before the winter sowing. This procedure was the basis of the more economical three-field rotation: winter corn, spring corn, fallow. This improved rotation was probably not even introduced into England until the eleventh century. Even then it superseded the earlier two-field rotation gradually and

* Attenborough, *Laws of the Earliest English Kings*, p. 49.

only on good soils. It was an important technical improvement, because it withdrew only a third, not a half of the village arable from use, but it was not a fundamental change in the mode of production. Long before it was prevalent the routine of open-field farming and manorial organization had crystallized.

The size of shares in the open fields normally proportioned claims to meadow, pasture, and woodland. The stock which normally went with a thirty-acre holding in the eleventh century was two oxen, one cow, a few sheep, and a horse. Although open-field farming brought about primarily improvements in agriculture, the care of live-stock continued to be important. Plough-oxen and horses were needed for work on the open fields and for transport; sheep were kept for their wool and their milk was used for cheese; cows' milk was used for butter and cheese; swine were the chief source of the peasants' meat supply. Until the development of large-scale production for the market, there was no incentive to feed livestock over and above the numbers needed for tillage, for peasant consumption, for the landlords' food supply, and for small reserves which could be handed over as rents and fines or exchanged for articles not produced in the village itself (iron and salt most notably). For peasants, in and after the pre-Norman period, normally grew their own food and made their own clothes. The village was almost self-sufficient. Methods of feeding livestock and of breeding were thus directed towards preventing the diminution of necessary numbers. Even so, advances were made. The waste and woodland provided rough grazing, especially valuable for swine. The land bordering streams and rivers was cleared and turned into grass meadows, mown each summer for hay. When the harvest was over the long stubble left standing in the fields provided food for cows and oxen and sheep. Part of the oats crop could be used as fodder for horses, which began to be employed in agricultural work during the early medieval period, although it was centuries before they entirely supplanted the ox as plough beasts.

Various subsidiary activities were carried on in the villages. Spinning and weaving, smithing, tanning and carpentry, baking and brewing and dairy work, were not yet specialized occupations; they were accessory to work in the fields. Most peasants probably kept hens or geese, collected honey, grew certain vegetables and herbs; in most regions they could fish and trap and hunt. (In the Fenlands fishing was a major industry.) But lords gradually monopolized fishing and hunting rights; and even in the seventh century we can see how they took toll of peasant food production through food rents. There is, for example, a passage in Ine's *Laws* defining a lawful food rent which a lord could take from an estate assessed at ten hides: "10 vats of honey, 300 loaves, 12 measures of Welsh ale, 30 measures of clear ale, 2 full-grown cows, 10 sheep, 10 geese, 20 hens, 10 cheeses or measures of butter, 5 salmon, 100 eels, 20 pounds of fodder." (About A.D. 694.)*

This food rent, like others exacted by private lords, was considerably heavier than the dues which the free lordless peasantry owed to the king. The transfer of the king's rights over land to ecclesiastical establishments and to thegns, was, it is safe to surmise, the starting-point in the subjection of the peasantry in a very large number of villages. And inequalities tended to become wider as the generations succeeded each other. In their development, open-field villages produced the rights of private property, the opposition between large scale landlord enterprise and the small property of an impoverished peasantry. Even in the pioneer stage, any member of a village community was free to monopolize a major share of the expanding village resources, if he could. So we hear of thriving, driving ceorls who prospered so that they had "fully five hides of their own land, church and kitchen, bell house and burgh gate";† thegns and ecclesiastics exercised similar rights of lordship, not within one or two

* Attenborough, *op. cit.*, p. 59.

† *Stubbs Charters* (ed. H. W. C. Davies), p. 88.

villages only but within scores. How had this come about? What was the effect on the structure of society?

Men and oxen in the pioneer phase of village activity were means of acquiring land. Villagers who had more oxen than their neighbours could, with the aid of their own dependents, obtain a larger share in the village fields without breaking away from the routine of the village community. Monastic communities would not only have reserves of cash with which to purchase oxen, if need be; they possessed a labour force in the humbler of their members; bishops or thegns who usually had slaves and a considerable number of peasant dependents, could develop a wide tract of land, reserving a large demesne for themselves. For royal grants of land were not always grants of settled land. In return for labour services, the slaves and peasant dependents would be hutted out on a portion of the land, dividing their labour time between their lord's demesne and their own acres. Even in the seventh century, Ine of Wessex and his witan found it expedient to regulate a lord's dealings with his tenants. He ruled that a tenant who received a yard land, that is a thirty-acre holding, from his lord, should pay only rent (probably a food rent, but possibly a rent payable in the form of money); but a tenant who received yard-land and homestead, and so probably plough oxen and other stock, should pay not only rent but labour service.* Here then is the evidence for the early embryonic existence of the typical landlord-serf relationship of the feudal age. It was growing up alongside the older, and in the seventh century still prevalent, system by which free peasants held land by folk right as an inheritance for their families, owing the customary tribal services to the king or the lord to whom the king had transferred his rights.

Lords, however, on receiving royal rights over land could exploit these public services in their own interests. They could intensify the burden of the food rent. They could build a mill and force the peasantry over whom they exer-

* Attenborough, *op. cit.*, p. 59.

cised a superiority to grind their corn at it, and deliver a portion of the corn by way of payment; such an exaction was the reason for building the mill. Similarly a communal oven or bakehouse, built for the village by the lord, brought profit to its owner, not the community who were obliged to use it. Lords could appropriate part of the woodland for their own use and then take toll of village pigs pastured in it. Even a parish-church, as we have seen, was provided by a lord as a means of attracting tithe and other payments from the peasantry.

Meanwhile the inheritance of free peasant families became smaller as the generations went by, and the original holding was divided among the children and divided again.* (But as life was insecure and early death frequent, the rules of inheritance sometimes worked the other way.) The less their resources the easier for peasants to be overwhelmed by any burden of rent which they carried, if misfortune came their way. And sooner or later disasters were sure to occur: a bad season, an outbreak of disease among the cattle, the imposition of a heavy judicial fine, total loss of cattle or crops by an enemy raid, or the action of thieves and outlaws. Prospering thegns, religious houses, the richer ceorls could survive all but the greatest disasters; but the ordinary freeman without rich kindred who would come to his assistance, went to a lord and surrendered his land into his hands, receiving it back on terms which, at best, placed him in the position of a tenant owing rent and service for his holding. After the ninth century this practice of *commendation* became very frequent. And whole communities of peasants could make a bargain with their lord, if they were unable to pay the communal food rent, placing in his hands the future control of their land and tenure. Churchmen, it should be noted, as careful and persistent engrossers of landright, were not averse to taking advantage of national disasters to increase their broad acres. Here is an example from the ninth cen-

* See above p. 20.

tury. A member of the Kentish nobility had agreed to pay a food rent to the monastery of St. Augustine in Canterbury. The record of this gift adds: "If it shall come to pass, as we hope it will not, that any panic should arise through a heathen invasion or any other calamity, so that it cannot be provided that year, then twice the amount must be given in the following year. Then if it still cannot be paid, three times the amount must be given in the third year. Then if he still cannot or will not pay it, land and title deeds are to be given to the community at St. Augustine's."*

In the century before the Norman Conquest and the years which immediately followed it, the creation of demesne farms in the villages, on which a number of peasant-tenants were compelled to labour in return for remaining in possession of land for their own subsistence, reached its climax. The imposition of Danegeld, and the Danish and Norman conquests were some of the external circumstances which helped to bring this about. Land, however, was useless without labour. Lords by no means wanted to reduce the condition of their peasantry to a uniform level of destitution; they wished to tie them to the land rather than drive them off. And it was in their interests for a proportion of their tenants to be in a position to maintain plough oxen and a horse. They also needed the services of free peasants and small thegns. Consequently the greater lordships of the eleventh century embraced different classes of men. They included men who were competent to assist the lord in the management of his estate, to fight under his banner in the host, and to escort him in his travels to the king's court or round his various scattered demesnes. The growth of lordships was indeed a vast social movement in which the tribal distinctions by blood and status were being superseded by the creation of a cleavage between the cultivators of the soil and men on whom the defence of the land and the maintenance of internal order rested. A man's rôle in society was

* F. E. Harmer, *English Historical Documents*, p. 45.

becoming fixed by the conditions or contract on which he held his land. Differentiation between a military class and a peasant class was never very hard and fast, even after the Norman Conquest. But documents of the eleventh century enable us to see how it had almost been achieved by that time.

For example, at the beginning of the eleventh century an estate agent of a great lord drew up a memorandum on how to deal with the groups of men within the estates of which the lordship was compact.*A fundamental distinction was made between the thegns who owed military and quasi-military services and the peasants. The former held land by book right; their services were to the king, their relationship to the lord was a personal relationship. The peasantry were subjects; the lord received their services. Of these the lowest group were *slaves*. For their work as permanent farm servants they received from the lord various allowances of food and an allotment of an acre. Labour on the lord's demesne was also performed by *cottagers* and *geburs*. The cottagers' economic position was precarious: they held only five acres of land, perhaps more; they were burdened with various services and dues, including one day's work on their lord's land. But they were not unfree, in the sense that slaves were unfree. They probably included impoverished descendants of the tribal peasantry or descendants of emancipated slaves, for throughout the Anglo-Saxon period lords had been liberating slaves in groups or as individuals. *Geburs* were in a more solid economic position; but their holdings in the land of a village, and the stock that went with them, had been given them by the lord; to the lord they returned on their death; and their services, varying from place to place, were considerably heavier than those of the cottagers: two days week-work, dues in kind, money renders, and various seasonal services and boon works. Whether of free

* Bland, Brown and Tawney, *English Economic History, Select Documents*, pp. 5-9.

or unfree descent, their condition reminds us of the
tenant-farmer of the seventh century, and was very near to
that of the serfs or villeins of the twelfth century. Finally
there were the *geneats,* a peasant aristocracy who, while
rendering money rents, dues to the church, and various un-
servile services to the lord, were, so we can surmise, either in
possession of land inherited from their free ancestors or land
held on lease from a lord. They were not tenants owing
servile services. As we can learn from Domesday Book, the
link which bound many peasants of free status to a lord
was not invariably irrevocable; some of them could "go with
their land" to another lord. And some of them had holdings
of more than thirty acres, sometimes considerably more.

Domesday Book was a digest of surveys made twenty
years after the Conquest which expropriated nearly all the
English thegns and replaced them by Norman knights and
barons. It is based on detailed information about the villages of nearly all England, collected by royal agents from
sworn statements of various local men. So it affords evidence
of the extent to which the villages had come under landlord
control. For the intention of the Conqueror was to obtain
information about the resources of the demesnes which he
claimed as royal land, of the great and small estates which
he had granted to his barons as fees, and of the estates he
had confirmed to the church. Shire by shire, estate after
estate, minute particulars were given of the manorial units
of which these estates were composed. From this great record
therefore we can make some rough estimates of the peasant
population and the stage which the competitive scramble
for estate property among the great ones of the realm had
reached by 1086.

The total population was probably under two millions.*
While the majority of the people lived on the land, towns
existed; markets or town dwellers were found in more than
a hundred places, and in a few of these places there were

* A. P. Usher: *Industrial History of England,* p. 89.

considerably larger concentrations of population than in the greater villages. The peasantry were well over 90 per cent. of the population and more than 75 per cent. were trembling on the brink of serfdom. Of these some were cottagers, men without plough-animals, others were men whose economic position in the village was not unlike those of the *geburs* in the document which we have referred to already. In certain shires there was still a considerable number of slaves, although in the total population of England they form a group of only nine per cent. In other shires, particularly in Lincolnshire, Norfolk, Sussex and Essex, the disintegration of peasant tenements had proceeded apace; even although there was a very high proportion of freemen or sokemen, the majority of the peasantry whether free or unfree in status, were economically in a wretched position, holding minute shares of arable and possessed of no oxen.

The division of estates among the ruling class can best be described in terms of the annual profits derived from them.* These, it is noteworthy, were estimated in cash:

The king and the king's family	...	£17,650
The king's sergeants	...	£1,800
		£19,450
Ecclesiastical tenants in chief, bishops, abbots, etc. (100)	...	£19,200
Earls and lay barons (170) ...	...	£30,350
English landowners (about 12)	...	£4,000
		£53,550

The way in which these great concentrations of manorial property were handled would clearly determine the next stage of economic and political development in England. For although Anglo-Norman civilisation was in a very immature

* *Cambridge Medieval History*, Vol. V, p. 508.

state in 1086, the ruling minority of landlords were politically strong and united enough to maintain their position of overriding power in the countryside; and although they enfeoffed many of their knightly followers, these new *feudal* tenants did not slip from their control.* Barons and knights until the later twelfth century were still essentially an alien occupying army ruling a conquered people. The subjection of the peasantry continued through the operation of the same forces as were at work before the conquest, reinforced by the effects of the Conquest itself. Slavery disappeared, slaves being absorbed into the ranks of the cottagers, into which impoverished villagers were constantly passing. Many more of the free peasants were depressed to the condition of tenant farmers or lost their freedom to betake themselves to another lord, although their numbers were supplemented by lords creating new holdings let out at a money rent. To the Normans all native villagers were regarded as unfree, as rustics, as serfs: tenants who should be excluded from the professions, and prevented from bearing arms. Freeholders, explained a lawyer in the reign of Henry I, should frequent the shire courts, but not "villeins, cottagers, farthingmen and low and needy persons of this kind; *viles et inopes personae*."† "Their's the dull routine of agricultural labour which a monk of the eleventh century symbolized in a dialogue written for schoolboys: §

"Ploughman, how do you work?

"—I go out at dawn to drive the oxen to the field, and yoke them to the plough. However hard the winter I dare not stay at home for fear of my lord—every day I have to plough an acre or more.—I have to fill the oxen's bin with hay and give them water and carry the dung outside.— Hard work it is because I am not free."

For the agricultural work services actually demanded from

* See below pp. 77-8.
† *Stubbs Charters*, Ed. H. W. C. Davies, p. 125.
§ *Aelfric's Colloquey*, Ed. G. N. Garmonsway.

serfs, manorial customaries are evidence.* On the whole the Normans exploited the peasantry more efficiently than their Anglo-Saxon predecessors, but this, as we shall see, was made possible by the expansion of exchange within the feudal social order.

To return briefly to Domesday Book. Detailed study of this record has made possible various observations worth keeping in mind as the development of English society after the Conquest is pursued. Widely as the population was now dispersed over England, there was still a vast amount of woodland. The greater stretches however, were monopolised as royal forests; and in these wide areas, which included peasant settlements, the pasture rights of the "beasts of the forest," had precedence. Savage game laws preserved them for the king's sport. Moreover the development of agriculture and the not necessarily co-ordinated process of the growth of demesnes, had been uneven. In the regions settled by the Danes, for example,† there tended to be a bigger proportion of freemen than in Wessex. North of Trent large tracts of land had been devastated by the Conqueror; there were few large demesnes, few religious houses; dales and fells formed a very primitive region until sheep farming was established in the mid-twelfth century. The Fenlands were also thinly populated. Consequently although the Norman clerks who made the drafts for Domesday Book saw manors everywhere, in estates in every part of England, they meant by the term little more than a unit within a landlord's property. Sometimes the core of a manor was a big demesne cultivated by dependant tenants. The demesne might lie scattered in the fields of one village only, but sometimes in those of adjoining villages; sometimes it lay within a ring fence; very often a single village contained more than one manor. In other cases a manor was more or less co-extensive with an old tribal region: there was little or no

* See below, p. 89.
† See below, pp. 63-4.

demesne, the landlord collected rents from the peasantry and held a court for them; such manors were common in the pastoral North. This may sound complicated; but to say the same thing in fewer words: in Domesday England the economic units were village communities, hamlets or outlying farmsteads. Manors were units of estates, sometimes, as we shall see, of quite small estates. The lord of an estate gained his living from his manors through the exploitation of the peasantry attached to them. Methods were very varied, and changed considerably in the two centuries which followed the Conquest. Before we can consider this development of the manorial system, it is obviously necessary to understand more clearly the social relationships within the ruling class after the Norman Conquest. How and why they had come about? Politics, we shall suggest, had as close a connection with economics, under feudalism, as in our own time.

CHAPTER V

THE PROBLEM OF ORDER

I

THE ideas and functions which we now associate with the word state are so complex that it requires some imaginative effort to understand a period when political institutions were embryonic and politics meant simply the organisation of defence, the suppression of rebellious vassals and the maintenance of order within the disintegrating local communities of tribal kingdoms. In the eighth century, tribal custom was no longer adequate in itself to prevent families who had built up a strong territorial position from defying the tribal king or domineering a local community. Feuds between rival kindreds, or within a single kindred, were serious affairs when the protagonists were powerful enough to assemble troops of well armed fighting men, accustomed to riding horses if not to fighting from horseback. A sentence of outlawry was of little use against a lord who could live by brigandage, or take refuge in a hostile land. And if it was a case of a great vassal defying the king, a single successful battle, and a kingdom might be won. It was in the light of the rich experience of eighth century struggles for personal power, perhaps on the continent as well as in England, that the poet who composed *Genesis* imagined the rebellion of Satan against God in heaven. He pictured Satan as an ambitious vassal, strong in the pride and strength of a great military following, next under God in the kingdom of heaven. So why should he serve? "I have great power to prepare a more splendid throne, higher in heaven" he reflects. "Why am I to wait upon his favour, bow before him with such homage? I can be a God as well as he. Strong comrades, bold hearted heroes, stand by me who will not fail in the fight; they, brave men, have chosen me for their master. . . . ."* Such might have been the calculations of any rebel warlord in actual contemporary history.

As events were to show, internal peace, and defence against invaders from abroad, could best be achieved within a realm which embraced all England, or at least England south of Humber. But a unified kingdom could only be built up and maintained if a number of landlords became conscious of their mutual need for collaboration, cohesion and discipline. Such consciousness was not easily, automatically, achieved. Normally the initiative in politics came from individuals, members of a royal or noble house. To maintain and extend their prestige and power, they needed not only the material support of efficient fighting men and prosperous peasants, but moral support: the force of the deeply rooted heroic tradition of the loyalty a man owed to his lord, and the more complex strength which could be gained by an

* *Anglo-Saxon Poetry*, p. 111.

alliance with the Church. On the continent, during the eighth century, Pepin and Charlemagne, the two most out-standing members of the Carolingian dynasty who seized kingly power over the Franks with the blessing of the Church, utilized and fused together incipient feudal and Roman-Christian traditions in their government with outstanding success. The state which they built up was an association of great military vassals, often *feudal* vassals, bound to the dynasty by ties of homage and fealty, integrated with the administrative system of the Church, which the Carolingians controlled. Frankish ecclesiastics accepted Carolingian rule as consecrated, God-ordained kingship; and the Carolingians in fact attempted not only to extend their dominions and break down tribal resistance in Saxony, but to foster the civilized arts in the monasteries and cathedrals of their extended realm and in the Palace. Given the circumstances, no other method of state building was practicable. If the co-operation of powerful vassals had not been gained, the magnates would have severally concentrated on consolidating their local power; prelates were prepared to support the strong man who would give them real protection against dis-orderly forces. But to govern through a professional bureau-cracy as the Roman Emperors had done, was out of the question in vast dominions where communications were difficult, literate men at a premium, and the possibility of raising taxes in money limited, or, in economically back-ward districts, neglible. Alfred of England, a king whose state building is comparable at many points to that of the Carol-ingians, summed up the relation of the king to his people in a homely and pregnant sentence; "A King's raw material and instruments of war are a well peopled land: and he must have men of prayer, men of war and work service men."* The weakness of this primitive political organisation lay in the difficulty of maintaining it when kings lacked

* Quoted in this translation by Moss, *Birth of the Middle Ages*, p. 271.

initiative on the battle field or in council. Without strong unified leadership, dominions dissolved into warring factions of nobles and prelates.

Alfred's achievement as king was stimulated by a crisis which effected the Frankish as well as the English dominions: the disaster, terror and doom of the Danish invasions, for doom it appeared to contemporary churchmen. The Viking phase in the expansion of the Scandinavian peoples, especially in its beginnings, threatened to engulf Europe, and to blot out Christianity by the piecemeal, oft repeated plunder of unprotected monasteries. Raiding war hosts cynically demanded tribute as the price of calling off a plundering expedition; sooner or later the forcible occupation of wide tracts of land for colonisation started. All this made it difficult to perceive that the Vikings were also opening up new routes along which commerce could flow. The first Viking raid on England, resulted in the sack of the monasteries of Lindisfarne and Jarrow, in 793-4. By 865, the Swedes had penetrated along the Russian rivers to the Black Sea; their ships appeared in force at the gates of the great city of Constantinople; Norsemen had occupied regions in Ireland, and the Isle of Man, whence raids were made on North West Britain. And the Danes, from whom Franks and English had most to fear, had established pirate bases at the mouths of the rivers Rhine, Scheldt, Somme, Seine, Loire and Garonne. They had even plundered the coast of Provence. When they met more effective resistance from the inhabitants of Western Europe than they had as yet experienced, a mass onslaught on England was planned. Seasoned by long campaigns, the Danish war bands (ships companies when at sea) occupied bases in East Anglia. For ten years after this first manoeuvre, the Danish host operated in England. Northumbria and Mercia quickly collapsed; the West Saxons fought back under the leadership of King Alfred and his brother. Soon Alfred was left as sole resistance leader. Then the Danish host began to disintegrate. In 876 Halfdan's men permanently occupied

Northumbrian territory, York being the centre of this Viking kingdom. Part of Guthrum's army settled in Eastern Mercia in the Trent Valley, in districts centring on their boroughs of Derby, Nottingham, Leicester, Lincoln. The rest of Guthrum's army continued the struggle for Wessex until Alfred drove them back on East Anglia, where in 879 they too made a permanent settlement.

In the years which followed, Alfred showed that he was a state builder of no mean quality. This scholar who enjoyed listening to tales of travel and puzzling over the mysteries of everyday phenomena, this pious, earnest king, had the ability to plan and the habit of reflection, traits more often found in monks than kings at this period. His laborious victory over Guthrum gave him an opportunity to organise defence by sea and land against further Danish ventures. Although he had not the power to drive the Danes from the settlements which they had already made in Eastern England, he prevented another Danish host from seizing London. In the English districts which now freely accepted his rule, he organised military districts centring on fortified places or boroughs, which were built and manned by the men of the regions in question. He also called on levies of peasant warriors for his military expeditions, as well as on his own thegns and those of the leading landowners; but he never summoned more than half the available peasants. Thus he was able to keep them on the field for long campaigns, while in the countryside the work of food production went on.

Meanwhile, in the midst of pressing needs of defence, Alfred attempted to restore the ecclesiastical civilisation which years of raids and incessant fighting had almost destroyed. Like Charlemagne he gathered learned men at his court. With their help he translated various Latin books into the English language, making additions and reflections of his own. He encouraged the continuation and diffusion of the Anglo-Saxon Chronicle, intending perhaps to reinforce the claims of his dynasty to rule over England. From his officials, including the ealdormen who ruled over the provinces of the kingdom, he expected intelligent co-operation, wanting them to share his appreciation for the learning of the Church and his own reflections on this world and the next. "I cannot find anything better in man than he know, and nothing worse than he be ignorant."* So they, and the sons of all substantial landowners, were to learn to read his English works. He was seeking to weave together the best of two traditions: that of the tribal past, in which "wisdom" and the language in which to express it was the heritage of all men, and that of the Church, in which the few gained knowledge by literary study. True, the social order which he visualized was built up on the basis of class distinctions. These were part of a divine order and necessary for civilized living. "Some dwell in cottages, some in halls . . . . and yet they all live by the favour of one lord, just as all men live under one sun and by its light see what they can."

In issuing a code of law to guide provincial doomsmen and officials throughout England, it was appropriate that he should preface his laws by a discourse on the Mosaic law: but he also digested the legal codes of dead tribal kings—Ethelbert of Kent, Ine of Wessex, Offa of Mercia—and tentatively made emendations: "I then Alfred king gathered these laws together and commanded those to be written which our forefathers held, those that seemed to me good, and those that seemed to me not good I rejected them by the counsel of my witan and ordained otherwise. For I dared not write much of my own. For it was unknown to me how that would please those that should come after us." In refusing subservience to obsolete custom he was taking a step forward. And in these revised laws, kindred loyalties were reduced to their narrowest scope, while tremendous

* This and other passages from the works of Alfred quoted below are found in Hodgkin, *History of the Anglo-Saxons*, Vol. II, Chapter 20.

stress was laid on the oaths of fidelity which bound a man to his lord. For on these depended the discipline of the army on the field and the maintenance of order in the provinces. The crime of treason against a lord was the only offence which a money fine would not amend.

II

Alfred's reign was the bridge which connected the age of Bede and Offa of Mercia with the work of the tenth century kings who consolidated an Anglo-Danish state.

Edward, Alfred's son, conquered the Danelaw, and incorporated its various districts within the English kingdom, without expropriating either the Danish nobility or the Danish peasants settled there. Viking power, however, was still on the increase in Europe as a whole, and the Danes in England were by no means Anglicised. Protection was still the crying need: protection against renewed Viking attacks, supported by Danes or Norsemen already settled in the island; and protection against thieves and robbers at home. For the dissolution of tribal discipline, hastened and aggravated as it had been by invasion and war, had set free all kinds of men from the customary bonds which had linked them to a particular social group or district. Society had to arm itself against the brigands it had fostered.

The rapid extension of landlord power was a spontaneous response to the conditions of the time. The economic side of this process we have already considered. But the binding of men to labour on demesne lands and the legal subjection of dependent peasants to the quasi-paternal authority of their lords, were interlocked movements which the tenth century kings not only recognised and permitted, but encouraged. A lord was responsible for disciplining his men, whether they were free or unfree peasants or domestic retainers. For example, following earlier legislation, Aethelstan enacted: "Every lord shall stand surety for his men against every breach of crime: if there is anyone who has so many men that he is unable to control them, he shall place each estate in the charge of a reeve whom he can trust, or who will trust the men."*

It was not enough to permit and sanction the growth of landlords' powers of jurisdiction over their men. The tenth century kings completed a drastic reorganisation of local government, and an even more drastic revision of the laws against thieves The folk regions of the various tribal nations were no longer adequate for the needs of the unified English kingdom. From the military point of view most of them were too small; from the point of view of dealing with criminals, settling disputes, and adjusting the burden of taxation between householders, most of them were too large. In any case the growth of economic lordship and the Danish invasion had dislocated the old system, so far as it survived. Gradually then, as royal responsibility for enforcing law and order was assumed, the greater part of the kingdom was redivided into districts which were no longer organic tribal units, but simply convenient administrative areas. Possibly the Frankish system of counties influenced the reorganisation. The shires were the largest subdivisions of the kingdom, roughly comparable to the counties of the Carolingian state.

We need not describe the process of formation, which in Wessex probably began before the reign of Alfred. Suffice it to say that the shires of England up to the Humber were in existence by the time of King Aethelstan. Their general lay-out can be seen in any political map of England. Each centred on a royal borough. Here were the headquarters of the earldorman, the king's official who led the shire both in war and peace. Here too was the assembly place for the thegns and other fighting men of the region. The thegns were now the dominant but not the sole element in any fighting force. At least twice yearly, a shire court or moot

* Attenborough, *Laws of the Earliest English Kings,* p. 145. Other laws quoted or referred to in this chapter are found in the same volume.

was held, which dealt with the king's business and disputes about land. Again the land owning thegns of the shire were, under the bishop and local magnates, the dominant element. They were the doomsmen, or declarers of custom and they witnessed the transactions carried out in the court. The shire, it should be noted, was the new unit for the administration of the king's demesnes, the specialized job of an official called the sheriff. Meanwhile smaller districts were being formed: hundreds in the English shires, wapentakes in the Danelaw. Most of them were subdivisions of the regions of the tribal kingdoms whose populations had been estimated in terms of hundreds of families. Like the older regional courts, the courts of these small districts assembled every month in the open air, dealing with business like the adjustment of the burden of communal renders of rent and taxation payable to the king, and the settling of pleas. On the hundreds was placed the duty of applying the new and desperate remedies for putting down thieves.

The enactment of these new laws is an illustration of the way the primitive machinery of state worked. England had no capital, no centre of government. The king and his household travelled up and down the kingdom, visiting in turn the chief royal manors, eating up their produce in so doing. At occasional intervals during these itineraries, there assembled councils in which the king met his prelates and leading thegns and chief officials from several shires, and secured their authority, consent and collaboration in the new measures for keeping the peace. Districts like the Northern Danelaw, which the king seldom or never visited, were, in practice, if not in theory, autonomous; there the king's writ* did not run.

The repression of brigandage, theft and violence was a complex problem. It involved dealing with the "great and

---

* The writ was a royal order, couched in the form of a letter, to one or more officials, or others. Its use started in the early eleventh century. Under the Norman kings and henceforward, sealed writs were used as a matter of course in every part of the king's government.

strong kindreds" who might stand up for their lawless men. It meant keeping track of desperate men who flitted from place to place; and also devising measures of controlling the sales of cattle, so that stolen animals could not be passed from hand to hand. To bring the criminal to justice, and at the same time to protect innocent men from malicious charges, was no easy task. The expedients actually adopted very clearly reflect a stage of social development in which, as tribalism disintegrated, kings perforce worked through the magnates and local communal institutions—the village and the hundred. These expedients are worth looking into because they help us to understand what kind of law and order was replacing tribalism in the tenth century; and they formed the basis of the criminal law of the Angevin period.

As we have said, the king recognised that lords should discipline their men. (Feudal lawyers accepted this right of "private justice" as axiomatic). Kindreds were ordered to find their unruly members a lord, if they could, and so make them amenable to law. Lords were also expected to bring their men to justice in the public courts, if they were accused of crime, or else suffer the penalty of a fine. They and the hundred reeves however, dealt with their policing problems by shifting the responsibility on to the peasantry. In every village tithing groups were formed: its members were expected to keep a watch on each other's movements. If one of them turned thief, the rest were expected to prevent him from making good his escape. (A fugitive from justice was *ipso facto* treated as a thief). They were expected to follow the hue and cry of the hundred after a thief who had left his trail. Again, if and when a man accused of theft was produced in court to rebut the charge—as was customary procedure—the court would not ask his kindred to swear to the truth of his denial, as formerly, but a group of neighbours, including one or two men of thegnly rank. If the accused had a bad reputation, he would go to the ordeal. In the Danelaw, and perhaps also in the English shires, a procedure very like that of the jury of presentment of the post-conquest period was followed: twelve leading thegns of the wapentake were summoned to indict on oath the men of the locality whom they suspected of crime. It is possible that the jury of presentment itself has its origin in the period: these jurors were a group of villagers, including the reeve and priest, who made a communal indictment of suspects in the hundred court. The point is of interest because this practice of forcing men from a locality to act as jurors kept the communal principle alive through the centuries of feudal rule; it constantly acted as a counterbalance to the bureaucratic tendencies of the feudal state.*

To return to the earlier tenth century: repression through savage punishments accompanied efforts to bring criminals to justice. A freeman guilty of theft was hanged, a woman of the same status was flung from a cliff or drowned; but slaves were tortured or burnt. The laws sanctioning the latter punishments were ingenious and detailed and suggest not only the existence of considerable numbers of slaves on magnates' estates, but also the possibility that slaves were a particularly lawless element. The stealing of cattle followed by flight doubtless offered a chance of self liberation. In any case Aethelstan ordered that each of a group of eighty slaves were to pay three pence to the owner of the guilty slave. They were then to stone him to death if he were a man; failure to aim effectively was punished with the lash. Women slaves were burnt at the stake. "If we relax this peace ordinance," the bishops and reeves who authorised similar penal measures in London solemnly declare, "then we may expect or rather know for certain that these thieves will have the upper hand even more than they did in the past." And children of over twelve might suffer, until towards the end of his reign Aethelstan spared children of under fifteen, "unless they resisted or evaded arrest . . . because he thought it too cruel to kill so many young people and for such small

* N. Hurnard, *The Assize of Clarendon,* English Historical Review, 1942.

crimes as he understood to be the case everywhere."
Eloquently the words indicate the terror that had been set
up.

Meanwhile justice was increasingly becoming a source of
profit to king and landlords. In the tribal period, crimes
had been amended by the payment of compensation to the
injured party. Gradually the practice of paying fines to the
king, or the lord, grew up. In the case of a man who had
been hanged, all his possessions were taken by the king, or
if he was under private lordship, by his lord. Kings granted
landlords immunities which in fact gave them the right to
hold private courts for their men; and in certain cases, in
the eleventh century, an abbot or bishop or other magnate
was licensed to hold the hundred court in districts where he
had considerable estates, and retain its profits. This process,
which in time might have diverted the machinery of justice
entirely into the hands of the great landlords, was in full
swing when the Norman Conquest occurred. It was of course
the almost inevitable accompaniment of the growing
economic subjection of the peasantry to the power of manorial lords, one part of the process by which the dependent
peasant was separated from all ties except those which bound
him to his exploiter. After the Norman Conquest we can
distinguish fairly clearly the two kinds of jurisdiction which
a lord might have over peasants. There was the jurisdiction
of the manorial court, in which offences against labour
discipline were punished, and business connected with the
holdings of peasant tenements dealt with and the payment
of peasant dues and taxes enforced. There was also franchisal
jurisdiction, in which the lord sat in the place of a royal
official and dealt with certain common crimes. It was the
latter type of jurisdiction which was most significant in the
late Anglo-Saxon period.

The Church in the unified kingdom of England was
closely bound to the king and his government. Alfred's dream

of a learned laity sharing with the clergy the delights of knowledge did not materialise. As Europe recovered from the devastation of the Viking invasions and began to profit from the trade which Viking enterprise helped to promote, monasticism revived and cathedral schools began to flourish. The profession of monk and the profession of learned clerk became means by which younger sons, with little or no share in the paternal inheritance, could find a stable place in society. Monastic reform began to influence England in the later tenth century. Thanks to the patronage of kings and nobles, monastic life and the literary activity of monks once again began to expand; but English still had an honourable place beside Latin as the language in which English monks wrote down their thoughts. In Western Europe, by contrast, Latin was almost exclusively used as the language of religion, law and learning. In Europe too were cathedral schools for secular clerks who, during the eleventh century, began to practise new methods in studying law and other subjects. As yet England had no share in this. There was, so far as we can tell, complete neglect of the study of Roman law; study of canon law was old fashioned. The Church in England was indeed insular; the life of its cathedrals and monasteries was rooted in the life of the surrounding districts. Rome was a distant place of pilgrimage whose Popes, at least until the eleventh century, had little more than a titular primacy. In this temporary eclipse of the Papacy, English bishops and abbots looked to the national king for protection; it was the king who nominated them to their Sees; it was the king from whom they received their lands; it was through the shire courts that the attention of the people was drawn to ecclesiastical laws which king and witan wished to enforce; it was in the hundred courts that the general disciplinary and administrative law of the Church was applied by bishop or archdeacon. At every level of its life the Church was identified with the king's government and landlord order. We need not be surprised therefore that paganism survived in English parishes far into the middle ages. The place of Christianity was not yet in the "hearts of the people". Up to the twelfth century it was in the monastery, in the courts of kings and magnates, in the cathedral, and in the towns, as they developed. But as town populations grew, so too did heresies and satiric criticism of the church system.

III

The Danelaw included some of the most prosperous regions of England in the eleventh century. In particular, commerce flourished there; for this was a time when Viking trade, centring in the Baltic, loosely linked together and enriched the scattered Viking colonies. In other respects however Danish power in England was not calculated to stimulate cultural progress. It tended to insulate England from the intellectual and political movements of Christendom. Thus the Danish dynasty who conquered England and ruled from 1016-1035 made no radical changes in either the territorial, legal or military organisation of the kingdom. Politically immature, Canute could learn something of the art of kingly rule from the English system, but could contribute few improvements. Hence the chief result of the Danish conquest of the eleventh century was to increase the already existing tension between the Danish and English nobility in England, and to shape, to some degree, the political situation in which the conquest of England by the Normans took place.

In Normandy, the French counterpart of the English Danelaw,* Danish settlers became the most effective element in the ruling class by absorbing the experience of the French

* F. M. Stenton in *The Scandinavian Colonies in England and Normandy,* in Transactions of the Royal Historical Society, (1945), seeks to explain the contrast between the "rustic conservatism" of the Danes in England, and the "passion for military adventure" of the Normans.

among whom they settled and with whom they fought and intermarried. Their warriors learnt the Frankish arts of fighting from horseback and castle building, and the co-ordinated military strategy. The current Frankish practice by which lords granted fees to their knights for their homage and service was adopted, a practice which, as we shall see, enabled customs to develop which bound the military class together for political as well as purely military purposes. In Normandy moreover agriculture and trade developed, for much of the land was fertile and its ports and towns lay close to important trade routes. Finally the rapid promotion of monastic life and learning by William of Dijon brought to Normandy eager students from Northern Italy and France to newly founded monasteries and schools. So Normandy, in the second half of the eleventh century, sheltered ecclesiastics who were anxious to promote reform of the Church along lines sanctioned by the canon law and the Papacy,* merchants with widely scattered trading interests, and knights and barons who, like their Viking ancestors, could be drawn into profitable military enterprise, although in action they were considerably more disciplined and formidable. Normandy was a small state; nominally its rulers were the vassals of the French king; but its civilisation was fully representative of all that was most progressive in contemporary society, and the reigning Duke, William, was a military leader and statesman of the first order.

These were factors which facilitated the Norman conquest of England. If we wish to explain why William of Normandy and not Harold, the West Saxon noble whom the English witan elected to resist the expected invasions, made good his claim to be the successor of the childless king, Edward the Confessor, then we must stress the statesmanship of William and the quality of the army he gathered together to share in the risks and rewards of his enterprise. Norman-French political experience and military skill counted, both

* See below pp. 108-9.

in the short and long run. With constructive purpose born of confidence in French civilisation, William the Conqueror and his men set about reorganizing the English realm whose nobility they had outwitted, defeated and expropriated. England became a colonial area for French knights and barons, for French merchants, for French monks and learned clerks. The Anglo-Danish nobility, in so far as they survived encounters with French cavalry, were nearly all in exile by the Conqueror's death; the Anglo-Danish peasantry, and some few degraded thegns, remained on the land subject to the French barons, knights and prelates, who took over the estates of the old ruling class. The peasantry therefore preserved the language and the traditions of the old English communities.

With the Conquest the long battle against the forces of disintegrating tribalism, both within and without the kingdom, came to an end. But the political changes effected by the Conqueror must not be exaggerated. William, as we can infer from his actions, had no wish to destroy the structure of the old English administrative system, or to lose any jot of power which belonged to the heirs of Edward the Confessor. So the writs of the old English chancery ran in his name. The law of the Confessor was applied as before in the courts of hundred and shire. The demesnes of the English king, with considerable accretions, passed into his hand; from them he claimed the dues owed by custom. He became the patron and protector of the English churches, on which he imposed *feudal* military service (although within set limits he allowed Norman churchmen, appointed to English bishoprics and abbacies, to reform the discipline of the clergy). So he acquired both the territorial and moral power to dominate even the most powerful of the magnates; to them he granted the forfeited estates of English thegns; he placed them in charge of shire courts, and of castles, which began to rise, at his orders, in all the strategic points of the realm. What was new in the Norman reconstruction of the English political system was the system of tenure by which these barons held their estates and by which they granted land to their own men.

It had long been realized, on the continent, that the centrifugal tendencies of a society dominated by territorial lords could be counteracted by the institution of the benefice or fee, which gave the tenant possession of a holding only so long as he performed the services which his tenure bore. The Conqueror in giving fees to his barons in England, thereby claimed overlordship of all the kingdom; his tenants, for their part, acknowledged their obligations to send an agreed number of knights to the army when called upon to do so, and to attend the king's court. The latter obligation was very important. A king relied on the co-operation of his men. To embark upon any major military action, or set in motion any political plan, without discussion, without securing the support of his magnates, would have been to court disaster. A tenant's refusal to pay military and political services was an act of treason, which by feudal custom merited forfeiture, exile or death. Moreover the king retained certain rights over the fees of his tenants in chief. These rights were acknowledged when the tenant died; his heir enjoyed the inheritance only after paying to the king a sum of money known as a *relief* and doing homage. If the heir was under age, the fee passed into the custody of the king together with the heir himself, until he was of an age to perform his due service. If there was no male heir, then the king would allow daughters to inherit, but only on condition that he arranged their marriages. In general, he controlled the marriage alliances made by his tenants in chief so as to prevent the formation of any combination hostile to his interests. If there was no heir, then the land *escheated*, that is passed into the king's ownership, until he chose to grant it to another. And the Norman kings also established precedents of demanding financial aid from their barons on certain specific occasions; and if, for some particular military expedition, kings preferred to have a money contribution from their tenants in lieu of personal military service, then they had the right to demand *scutage*—a sum of money levied on each knight's fee, assessed on the basis of the cost of maintaining a knight in food and fodder for the customary term of service.

Such was the custom of the kingdom as it developed in the period from 1066 to 1135, the year which marked the death of William's youngest son, Henry I. This tense and regulated *feudalism* was not the Conqueror's personal achievement. It was built up with the consent of his barons. The Anglo-Saxon chronicle, it is true, tells us that no one dared to withstand the will of the Conqueror: "the rich complained and the poor murmured, but he recked nought of them; they must all will what the king willed, if they should live or keep their lands or hold their possessions or be maintained in their rights." But the precarious position of the Normans in England created among the barons a sense of class solidarity, of cohesion in the face of common danger. For the possibility of a Scandinavian invasion, linked with an English uprising, that is repetitions of the Hereward episode, were omnipresent in the first generation after the Conquest. And any weakening of the Norman position in England would be, and in fact was, an opportunity for the French king to threaten Norman possessions in Normandy. Hence baronial support for their king and military leader, their loyalty to all the customs which fostered military efficiency and mutual solidarity.

The leading barons tended to reproduce the tenurial system created for the kingdom within their own estates, or, to use a characteristically *feudal* term, honours. While retaining knights and sergeants for their immediate domestic needs, for great barons, like the king, travelled with a retinue of knights and employed laymen with knightly skills in the administration of their estates, barons normally provided for the knight service they needed to fulfil their obligations to the king, by granting fees to their vassal knights. From such knightly tenants and from all freemen to whom they granted fees, they exacted the same kind of service, as they themselves owed to the king. In the courts which they held for transacting the business of the honour, they sought the support and consent of their greater men, as the king did of them. The same sense of community which normally existed between the king and his chief tenants, existed also between the lord and the greater tenants of a baronial honour. In defending their rights against the lord, tenants of an honour might appeal to the custom of the honour in just such a way as the king's barons appealed to the custom of the realm. And when, as did Henry I on his coronation, a king endeavoured to canvass the support of his great tenants in chief by a formal recognition of what was regarded as good *feudal* custom, the barons in their turn recognized their obligation to apply similar principles in dealing with their own tenants.

The tenant of an honour however was not entirely outside the king's reach. The king was his supreme lord, in the sense that he owed obedience to the lord of his fee only in matters which did not cut across his duty to the king of England. He not only attended the court of his lord, he attended the courts of the kingdom, and in particular the shire court. Of necessity the king relied upon baronial sub-tenants as well as his own barons to support the sheriff, his official, in running the shire court, as thegns had collaborated with the old English officials. (Many native English freeholders during the early twelfth century were, as we have seen, following the downward trend into serfdom). For the Norman kings, the maintenance of the old English system of local government was all important. Only through so doing could they retain control of the crown lands and regalian rights,* and keep their initiative in the administration of justice and the collection of taxation. The balance of power as between king and magnates would have been completely changed if baronial families secured *hereditary* rights over sheriffdoms, similar to those they possessed in their fees. The possibility of such a feudalisation of the shires emerged in the reign

* See below p. 113.

of Henry I, the second generation after the conquest; and it was, for the time being, successfully countered by the crown. Henry I chose sheriffs largely from non-baronial families; he intensified central control over sheriffs by instituting the Exchequer, and placed justices at their side to hear the pleas of the shire court, so incidentally raking in profit for the king's exchequer more efficiently.*

The tension created by Henry I's policy led directly to the feudal reaction of Stephen's reign. With two claimants to the crown, Stephen and Matilda, "every man did what was right in his own eyes", or more specifically, some of the greater barons bargained with one or both of the rival claimants for royal power for hereditary control of local government offices. Geoffrey de Mandeville for example, a great magnate in Essex and surrounding counties, blackmailed Stephen and Matilda in turn for the hereditary sheriffdoms and justiceships of Essex and Hertford, London and Middlesex and the office of Constable of the Tower of London. Meanwhile in various key districts civil war raged; the gendarmerie of certain castles, often mercenaries imported to fight out the question of succession, reduced the countryside to misery. So the latent contradiction between a military aristocracy at loggerheads with each other and an agricultural economy was again revealed; even within the feudalism of post-conquest England lurked the possibility of temporary anarchy, if and when the solidarity of the baronage round the king was broken. But nothing more clearly illustrates the political sense of the Anglo-Norman ruling class, than the speed with which they accepted a king pledged to restore the regulated feudalism of Henry I. (1153-4.)

So by 1154 the initial phase in the growth of the feudal state was over. The problem of defence, the problem of securing internal order, both as against the peasantry and as among the members of the ruling class had been solved.

* See below pp. 116-7.

At least all concerned understood the system which they maintained or under which they suffered. Better expanding revenues than diminishing plunder. Irrevocably by 1154 the defenceless, hardworking peasantry were subject to the will of lords who were discovering the possibilities of changing customs which cut across their economic interest, not only by the local imposition of their will, but by political collaboration with the crown. By 1154, as we shall see in the next chapters, the growth of exchange was already changing many methods of exploiting both manorial and *feudal* rights.

CHAPTER VI

GETTING AND SPENDING

THE slow and troubled, but not blind and mechanical process which brought feudalism into being, had its climax in a phase of confident, many-sided progress. In England this roughly coincided with the twelfth and thirteenth centuries. Both in England and Europe potentially anarchic social elements, including land-hungry peasants and the younger sons of knights and magnates, were absorbed into activities which, on the whole, increased the wealth of society and immensely enlarged its opportunities. Within the territorial states formed in the early middle ages, kings and princes enforced their peace ruthlessly enough to allow agriculture and commerce to progress. The conquest of backward lands on the Celtic-Scandinavian or Slav fringes of feudal Europe; commercial and territorial expansion in the Eastern Mediterranean under the guise of Crusades; the growth of towns as centres of trade and industry; the rise of new religious orders, and of secular schools for the study of letters, law, theology, medicine: these were some of the movements which provided an outlet for the rising population of

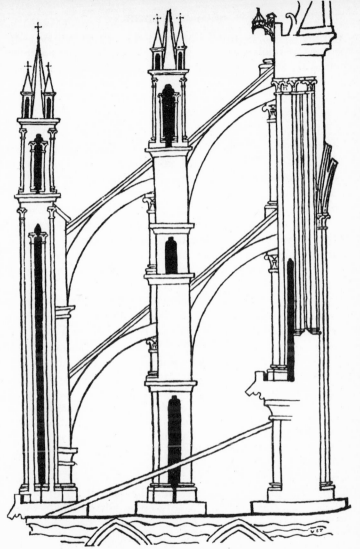

From sketch book of Villard de Honnecourt.

81

Europe. Reacting upon and modifying the primitive institutions of feudalism, they helped to shape a more complex
and diversified society, with a superficial unit of culture and
institutions.*

I

The complex and changing social pattern of English life
in the heyday of feudalism has its own logic, arising from
the interaction between economic life and the social needs
and ambitions of the ruling class. In other words, the everyday business of the production of food and other articles of
consumption, should not be set on one side in a study
of social development. For without the work of peasants,
other social groups, including those indispensable allies of
the great landowner, the professional administrators and
lawyers, the skilled craftsman, the merchant and the money-
lender, would not have secured a livelihood. Without increased rural production there would have been no flowering
of culture in monasteries, in feudal courts, in cities. That
peasant labour maintained feudal civilisation was a common-
place even in the middle ages. It should be taken seriously.

Many factors old and new combined to increase the output
of rural products in England during this period. In the first
place population was increasing. If estimates of population
vary, they agree on this point. Hence with renewed impetus
the extension of arable and pasture lands proceeded, and new
settlements were formed. For in 1086 there was still much
uncultivated or thinly settled land, especially north of the
Trent and Dee. And even in regions where the population
was less scanty, there were still considerable stretches of
woodland; lowlying marshes could be secured for tillage or
pasture by embankment. Nearly every village had a more
or less extensive hinterland of downland or heath adjacent
to its fields. It was possible therefore to extend simultaneously

* This point is taken up in the next chapter.

both pastoral farming and agriculture. In addition to this extension of farmland, there were also some minor improvements in traditional farming methods, especially in sheep and dairy farming, but nothing that can be called an agricultural revolution. The balance between corn-growing and stock-raising maintained in any particular group of settlements, was still largely determined by the nature of the land. Each community of peasants lived, as before, mainly of its own, but there was some outflow of surplus peasant production to the markets. A great deal of labour was concentrated on working the arable demesnes of the crown, the churches, the lay magnates, and lesser barons and knights, and landlord production of corn for the market became systematic; on many estates there was highly organized large-scale commercial production of wool and cheese. Rural industry also developed: stone quarries, lead and tin mines, iron works, salt pans, surface coal workings, mills for fulling cloth, fisheries. Much of the produce was marketed; and although manorial bailiffs seldom managed these little enterprises themselves, the cash rents paid by leasees formed an appreciable part of manorial profits in the parts of England affected by this development.

Production of food and the raw materials of industry for the market was only one side of the system of exchange which was developing within England, drawing the great estates into the orbit of an expanding European commerce. It is not part of the plan of this chapter to attempt a discussion of the origins and development of European commerce. Space is too limited; obviously it would be better for the reader to refer to one of the standard accounts of this vast subject.* But before we begin to discuss the interactions between this exchange economy and the feudalism of the early twelfth century, we should at least be clear that there had been no pure *natural economy* in Western Europe at any time during the dark ages; in England there is every indication that com-

* For example, H. Pirenne, *Economic and Social History of Medieval Europe,* (1936).

merce was already beginning to impinge upon rural economy and estate management before the time of Domesday Book.

The older writers on English economic history took a different view. Ashley, for example, thought that a money economy became significant only as the manorial system began to disintegrate in the fourteenth century. The beginnings of the transition from a "natural economy" to a "money economy" in the period 1000-1300 were inconsiderable; natural economy prevailed outside the towns. Such formulae are misleading; the facts discovered by later research on the period before 1300 cry out against them. So manifold were the money transactions of the thirteenth century that they have driven some of the historians who have drawn attention to them to the opposite extreme of concluding that capitalism itself was already in existence; so adding confusion to confusion, by equating capitalism with the drive for expanding cash revenues from serf-run estates, with credit, usury, and the large-scale production of wool and corn for the markets. Certainly in a few towns of thirteenth century Europe, the more important industries had come under the control of merchant capitalists, but these were operating within a feudal economy; they were not the dominant figures in economic life.

On what ground should we abandon the antithesis of natural economy and money economy in connection with feudal society? First, let us glance at the period before 1086. After the migrations, even in Germanic regions like England, coined money was used to measure values: cows and oxen, for example, as well as human beings, had their cash equivalents. Coins could be exacted from peasants as rent; they could be used in transfers of estates or goods. True, as we have seen, rent was usually paid in labour or kind; plunder, rather than trade, was frequently a way of obtaining cattle or precious articles. A man's status was increasingly dependent on his landed estate. None the less, the tendency for money to be used more frequently, and for peaceful traffic to supersede plunder, was predominant.

As the commerce characteristic of the Roman Empire, radiating from Mediterranean cities, declined, European traders became more active. They established headquarters in old Roman towns and fortresses, or in new boroughs (fortified places). The Venetians by the tenth century were becoming the principal middlemen between Constantinople and Italy. Lombards, encouraged by the peace imposed by the German Emperors over Italy, Germany and Burgundy, trafficked over the Alps into the Rhineland. Meanwhile, mainly through the activity of Flemish and Scandinavian traders, trade routes were being formed along the great rivers of Northern Europe and across the Northern seas. There was a trade route along the Danube to the Rhine. Trade to and from the Baltic and the Mediterranean flowed by way of Novgorod and Kiev. The first expansion of population occurred in towns which were in close contact with these principal trades routes; for example, in towns like London, York, Norwich in Eastern England. By the eleventh century European merchant business had acquired the two-fold character which was in the future to enable the use of money to penetrate downwards into the roots of the social system. Merchants, in addition to a primitive traffic in slaves, furs, eastern luxuries, and goods with a scarcity value, bought food and the raw materials of industry from country markets, or from traders who had dealings with such markets, for sale to dwellers in city or borough. And they handled commodities manufactured in Europe: wine, for example, or cloth, linen, glass, and other work of urban craftsmen. For this international trade stimulated specialization of production; it was supplementary to the local trade of peasants, which is so dark a subject. It is clear that it revolved round the great landlords, in so far as the main supplies of rural produce came from their manors, at first in an irregular haphazard way, as unexpected supplies became available; and from their sales they obtained the cash to purchase the means of living ceremoniously.

In England, these forms of exchange were developing as the

great estates were being formed. Cities and boroughs, like manors, were under landlord rule; manorial markets were established as part of the estate economy. As the trading-artisan populations of these various marketing centres increased, the settlements lost something of their original semi-agricultural character. Borough tenements within the walls were multiplied; burgage rents, which were cash rents, accordingly increased. So too did the profits from market tolls. And in addition to augmenting the cash revenue of lords, the markets of manors and boroughs formed a profitable outlet for manorial produce. It is not surprising, therefore, that kings and magnates played an important part in developing this aspect of their demesne rights; especially kings. So trading outside markets was forbidden. Kings firmly controlled the pattern and weight of coins. Standard measures and weights, if not national, were regional. Money was sufficiently dispersed for kings, in the eleventh century, to draw from all the realm a money tax on land. When in 1086 the king set in motion the great Domesday Survey of the estates of his kingdom, the value of manors was estimated not only in terms of their arable, pasture, stock and labour, but in terms of their cash values (perhaps a sum including annual money rents, assessed value of demesne crops and stock, and other manorial assets). Already the king drew annual money rents, not annual food quotas, from the farmers of most of the crown manors. The rent was traditionally supposed to be a sum equivalent to the price of the stock, corn, fodder, etc., included in the former food quota.* No change shows more clearly how inappropriate is the term "natural economy" to the manorial regime of the eleventh century. The king had freed himself from the routine of travelling round the royal manors to feed his household. This meant that the men who managed his very considerable demesne manors were disposing of some rural produce locally; while the royal house-

---

* The passage from the *Dialogus de Scaccario* about the commutation of food rents is quoted in translation by R. Lane-Poole, *The Exchequer in the Twelfth Century*, pp. 62-64.

hold purchased some at least of the supplies it needed. We can also infer that magnates and religious houses maintained the older system of food quotas not out of necessity, but out of lethargy or convenience. As we shall see, its maintenance, or partial maintenance, during the next two centuries did not prevent them from also producing for the market. These, then, were some of the ways in which money entered into the ordinary affairs of king and magnates in the eleventh century and earlier; money was an integral part even of primitive feudal economy.

II

As vital evidence has been lost, it will never be possible to write a full statistical history of the effects in England of the expansion of commerce during the twelfth and thirteenth centuries. As things are, it is possible to collect only fragmentary and elusive material for showing how different groups of landlords manipulated their manorial rights to acquire more cash to spend. It is still more difficult to show in detail how this revenue was spent. Two general considerations, however, should be enough to indicate that the first problem was necessarily complex. First there was the very heterogeneous character of the manorial system, which varied from region to region and from estate to estate, and so, in a large scattered estate, from manor to manor; and second, there was the rapidly changing commercial environment of Europe.

The way in which a manor would be managed depended partly on the local custom of the manor in which a long history of landlord-peasant relationships had already crystallised, partly on the will or purpose of the lord—the lord imposed by the Norman settlement, or a subsequent act of enfeoffment. Obviously estates in pastoral Northumbria, on which there were no large demesne farms, only semi-tribal communities of peasants rendering food rents and free services at a seignorial hall, were a different proposition from

the agricultural villages of the fertile midlands, where numbers of peasants were subjected to the demands of big arable
farms, run by manorial officials. Moreover different types of
landlords had different needs and varying capacity of enforcing their will. If the lord was a king, a bishop, or a great
baron, he had greater administrative capacity of enforcing
changes than a lord of humbler status. Very often he exercised over his tenants franchisal jurisdiction as well as ordinary manorial discipline. Manors which had long been incorporated into an ecclesiastical estate had behind them deep
rooted custom, already well adapted to the purpose of supplying food to a religious community. On the other hand, the
head of a pioneer religious community like a Cistercian
abbey, lord of undeveloped tracts of hill country, restricted
by the rule of his order from obtaining income from the
usual manorial sources of profit, would perforce respond
quickly to the opportunity of getting rich through the sale
of wools: hence his concentration on the organisation of big
sheep farms, supervised and worked by lay brethren. Finally,
the small landowners with annual incomes round about the
£10 level, were in a very different position from their feudal
superiors. Their tenements could be managed by themselves,
for they normally lay near each other, in one or two villages.
They were very often short of serf labour; for a share of the
villeinage, the land of the village allotted to tenants owing
labour services, was not necessarily included in every grant of
freehold. Hence the small landowners, and also the prospering peasant, relied upon undersettlers or cottagers for much
of the necessary labour on their home farms.

So far as the manors of magnates and the older religious
houses were concerned—and until recently little was known
of manors except those on the estates of monastic communities—expedients for increasing the cash due from them,
varied with the changing economic circumstances. Those of
the twelfth century, before the great producers' boom of the
thirteenth century had reached its climax, are least well
known. Colonisation was proceeding; peasants were moving

to the new lands, or into the towns. For, as even the lawyer Glanville acknowledged, town air made free. As the holders of great estates continued to enfeoff tenants, as subinfeudation and the exchange of freeholds enabled newly established small landlords or religious houses to consolidate and extend their estates from the original nucleus, a considerable broadening of the manor-owning class took place. On the whole however there seems to have been no equally significant or proportionate extension of peasant tenements. This is one of the very obscure questions. Certainly, however, in those shires where a considerable body of free peasants survived the Conquest into the later twelfth century, peasant grants to newly founded religious houses were considerable. It is difficult to believe that peasants granted away their livelihood out of pure piety; economic compulsion seems the more likely reason. Behind the grants of both peasants and gentry, in more cases than we know; there perhaps lay a tale of some debt which the religious house undertook to pay in return for rights over a particular tenement or of some other conditions, the details of which have been lost. In their landlord capacity, religious houses do not seem to have been popular. Satiric comment of courtiers, in the twelfth century, begins the attack which later on is developed by the ballad singers. A knight who had pledged and lost his land to St. Mary's of York was a suitable recipient of Robin Hood's assistance in the *Little Geste of Robin Hood*.

A few surveys of the lands of religious houses made in the late twelfth and thirteenth centuries have survived: testimony to the recognition by landlords of the benefits of keeping business-like records of the rents and services due to them from the tenantry of their manors. From these records some generalisations about changing methods of estate management have recently been put forward.* In the twelfth century, it has been suggested, demesne cultivation was declining and some labour services were commuted into cash rents; while

* M. Postan, *Chronology of Labour Services*, T.R.H.S. 4 Series, 1937.

in the thirteenth century demesnes were extended and labour services intensified. How true is this?

Clearly there was a tendency for lords to rent out, for cash, acres of newly cleared land; sometimes they also rented out or leased some acres of the demesne. The tenants who took up such holdings however, were not necessarily peasants; many would be gentry, lords of manors with a substantial number of acres already under their control. Valuation of various kinds of agricultural works in money, followed by lords forcing tenants owing labour services to pay the cash equivalent for any services not required of them, may be an indication that less labour was needed on demesnes, and that consequently they were "declining". On the other hand, it was sometimes convenient to utilize the labour of cottagers and undersettlers. There are also cases of a lord leasing the whole demesne farm to his customary tenants for an annual cash rent, which left the villagers free to manage their fields without the supervision of bailiffs from the lord's household, at least for so long as this arrangement held good. Commutation of food dues and occasional labour services were also common in backward districts where primitive conditions lingered. All these however were so many ways of extracting cash rather than food out of manorial rights. They do indeed suggest that manorial exploitation was being brought up to date, but not that the system itself was disintegrating. In any case the evidence only relates to the holdings of ecclesiastical houses; the readjustments were not intended to be permanent in every case; certainly they do not prove that lords were willing to allow their rights over their tenants to lapse. On the contrary, the significant development of the twelfth century was the depression of large numbers of peasants to serfdom or villeinage, and the emergence of a legal theory of their unfree status. For Glanville,* their characteristic disabilities were first, their absence of right

---

* Or, at least, for the author of the twelfth-century treatise on the English Common Law usually ascribed to Glanville, who was one of the justices of Henry II.

to appeal to the king for justice, and second, their absence of right over their own chattels and holdings. Both disabilities made them helpless victims of fiscal exploitation. A lord could tallage his villeins at his will: he could exact fines from them, by reason of their unfreedom. A villein could not purchase his own freedom with his own cash. He could not marry his daughter without paying *merchet*. His sons could not inherit the holdings of his father without paying *heriot*. No members of the villein's brood could leave the manor without paying a yearly sum, *chevage*. How profitable were such lordly rights to dip hands into the pockets of a villein we do not know. Events in the thirteenth century, however, tell us that whether a villein did his labour services or paid cash for them, was a matter for his lord to decide. He was still a villein.

The twelfth-century tendency for landlords to treat the villein as a cash-producing tenant was certainly succeeded by a tendency for big landlords to exploit his liability to labour services. For Bracton,* in the mid-thirteenth century, the villein- could be employed in any job which the lord wanted done. For in the thirteenth century some demesne farms of great landlords, far from contracting, were expanding. The Cistercian monasteries in the later twelfth century had been pioneers; they had shown how profitable large-scale wool production could be. Prices for wool and food stuffs were rising in the later twelfth century,† a price movement which continued into the thirteenth century, apparently in response to the insistant demand for these commodities from the rising towns, especially the Flemish cloth towns, expanding far more rapidly than the towns of England. Good prices and an assured market seemed to have acted as an incentive to increased production. Provided that the great landlords could place their manors and stock under competent bailiffs and devise a workable system to prevent

---

* King's justice, author of a treatise on the Common Law of England.
† W. Beveridge, *The Yield and Price of Corn in the Middle Ages*, Economic History, 1927, p. 164.

them from cheating, they could in normal years make good profits from large-scale demesne farming. Relying then upon a hierarchy of officials, a council to advise stewards, stewards to supervise bailiffs, bailiffs to supervise the elected serf officials from the manors, who were overseers of the tenantry, great landlords plunged into the business of production for the market. Demesnes were extended through taking in new clearings and vacant holdings. Where the land was sufficiently fertile a three-field system replaced the two-field system in open field areas. Labour services were exacted in full, even from tenants whose services had previously been entirely commuted for cash payments. On some estates villein tenements were divided without decreasing the service due from each tenant. On others, extra services were introduced and enforced. It is true that on most big manors a few permanent farm servants, paid by allowances of food and money were maintained; (their jobs were similar to those of the slaves on the pre-conquest estates). In rush periods task workers could be employed, but usually the whole body of the tenantry, man woman and child, were mobilised to . pay traditional boon works; for, on the whole, the high demesne farming of the thirteenth century depended on an intensification of customary labour and carrying services. Within this traditional system, an attempt was made to organize production for the market as efficiently as possible.

Manorial records, and treatises like that ascribed to Walter of Henley,* show that bailiffs were not afraid of piling arduous tasks upon a recalcitrant peasantry, if they were convinced that this would increase output. "Because customary servants neglect their work it is necessary to guard against their fraud". So, honestly enough, Walter of Henley lays down a key principle of estate management. At the same time traditional techniques were tested by the criteria of whether or not they increased profit and were efficient. A plough team of oxen with two horses was better than a

---

* Walter of Henley's *Husbandry,* Ed. E. Lamond, (1890).

plough team of horses only, which customary servants would not follow with suitable zeal; marl should be mixed with dung to make a good fertiliser; "corn seed grown on other ground will bring more profit than that which is grown on your own"; stock should be carefully sorted out each year and if necessary beasts should be fed with oats or peascods. (The growing of legumes was a progressive feature of late thirteenth-century agriculture). In pastoral districts the care of stock was usually placed in the hands of an official directly responsible to the lord's high steward; very large flocks of sheep were built up, and, especially in areas where there was much meadow pasture, large herds of cows. Cows were also pastured in woodlands; so too were horses. Royal and seignorial sheep farms, dairy farms, stud farms, vied in efficiency with similar pioneer establishments of Cistercian monasteries. Royal lordship over the forests acquired a new significance and aroused sharper antagonisms.

Bailiffs disposed of corn, cheese, butter from their lord's farms as was convenient. From the later twelfth century continental firms of merchants were very active in England, especially in buying wool from the large scale producers, for sale in Flemish or North Italian cloth towns. They made contracts with them for so many sacks of wool, for so many years, and paid cash in advance of supply, credit transactions which tied the producers closely to them and often obliged producers to buy up local supplies of wool to make up the agreed quota. In accounting for the slow development of the English urban cloth industry, this diversion of the bulk of the English wool crop to competitor towns overseas is of major importance.

The intensified pressure on the labour time of serfs, characteristic of the big estates in the richer agricultural regions, seemed all the more oppressive because on smaller estates the peasants with average sized holdings were often relatively free from labour services. If their holdings were large enough, they produced not only for themselves but for the local market. In agricultural villages which had been

divided into many manors through the process of subinfeudation, the total acreage farmed by the holders of large freeholds (over 50 acres) might be very high relatively to the
land used by the peasantry; but peasant labour services
tended to be insignificant. Let us see for example what the
position was in the village of Henry de Bray: Harlestone in
Northamptonshire. This we can assess because Henry de
Bray, like his betters, chose to keep an estate book.* He was
perhaps the most important resident landlord in his village;
but he held his tenements of the three non-resident lords
whose fees in Harlestone were units of much larger estates.
Henry de Bray had a demesne farm of some 250 acres and
about twenty-three tenants. The more important of his
tenants owed him only money rents; some, in addition, boon
works in harvest time. While six held of him tenements of
thirty acres or more (and it is quite possible that they held
tenements of others too), five held under five acres, five held
cottages only; they too owed cash rents and boon services.
From these poor peasants Henry de Bray probably recruited
his labourers, paying wages in food and cash. He was living
at the height of the boom period; he received just over £10
yearly in rent alone, apart from what he acquired from the
sale of surplus demesne-produce, probably in the near by
market of Northampton. Part of the profits of his estate
were expended in improving his farm buildings, as well as
on the amenities of his manor house. In short Henry de
Bray's management of his single manor was efficient and
progressive and different from the method which he would
have adopted if he had been the bailiff of a group of
seignorial manors where the problems of managing serfs and
extracting maximum cash profits were primary.

And he was no isolated phenomenon, at least in the prosperous agricultural regions of England. He was typical of
the whole rising class of gentry and free-holders. For with
considerably less capital and land, a prosperous peasant

* *Henry de Bray's Estate Book*, (Ed. D. Willis), T.R.H.S., 1916.

would manage his affairs in much the same way. Kosminsky, the Soviet historian, has shown that the manors of small landowners formed enclaves among the manors of magnates.* When the boom in high demesne farming collapsed and the great demesne farms were partitioned, estates like those of Henry de Bray were able to weather the period of slump, and eventually were adapted to the ways of the capitalist squirearchy of the sixteenth and seventeenth centuries. For in the late thirteenth century their economy was already adapted to conditions where there were impoverished peasants and an outlet for farm produce on the home market.

To generalise, then, on the state of the peasantry about 1300, is difficult. On the great estates, many serfs, in accepting their burdens, did so with an undercurrent of passive resistance. On the whole, serfs tied to labour service on a big demesne farm, held larger holdings and consequently had more security than the majority of the peasantry in villages dominated by resident gentry or a few prosperous peasants. Everywhere landless peasants or undersettlers were increasing in numbers, but especially in the latter type of village. Some engaged in rural industry; the rest formed a reserve of labour on which both prospering peasants and lords of manors could draw. Freedom from labour services gave both serfs and free peasants extra time and energy to devote to their husbandry. Legal freedom was of importance; for free peasants were more secure than unfree from the arbitrary taxation and fines of manorial lords. But where peasants, whether legally serfs or not, were producing for the market, the odds were against them; failure more likely than success. For they were handicapped by lack of the cash resources derived partly from feudal rents, which enabled the gentry or big landowners to survive bad seasons or to purchase land or to buy up stock.

Peasants and gentry, about 1300, were unable to expand

* Kosminsky, *Rents and Labour Services*, Economic History Review, Vol. V, No. 2.

their activities because of the continued existence of the vast sheep farms and big arable demesnes of the great magnates and churches. Landhunger was perhaps the most universal peasant experience. It nourished peasant consciousness of class oppression as effectively as the more dramatic occasional conflicts between serfs and manorial officials. Sometimes passive resistance against forced labour services flared up in a brief act of violent rebellion, but more usually, peasants burning with a sense of injustice would try, like their free neighbours, to get legal redress. They would draw up a list of grievances, and if they had any loophole for so doing, appeal to the king.* But as a general rule the king's judges gave no hearing to the pleas of serfs. Their justice was for freeholders. The place of serfs in feudal society was as stock in their lord's keeping. The external sanction to serfdom as exploited in the late thirteenth century was the judge-made common law; and the refusal of the king's judges to protect villeins against manorial oppression had its logical consequence later on in their failure to protect them against eviction.

III

On the whole landlords spent their incomes without investment in commercial enterprises outside their manorial estates. Like all generalisations, apparent exceptions to this can be found. Richard Duke of Cornwall, for example, whose vast revenues were partly derived from his Cornish tin mines, financed the new coinage of 1247-8 for a half share of the profits. A few years later however he was pouring out his treasure and income in a foreign adventure, as so many feudal princes before and after him had done, or were to do. On the whole then the big feudal landlord let his money run through his hands. It was spent in various ways: in provisioning, clothing and paying his household, (paid services were increasingly taking the place of services owed

* For example, see R. H. Hilton, *A thirteenth century poem on disputed villein services*, E.H.R. 1941.

by feudal contracts in the thirteenth century); in great building works—castles, cathedrals, monasteries, country houses; or in lawsuits, military adventures and the expensive diplomacy and outlay which the latter involved. Directly or indirectly, this spending business stimulated the growth of towns, the headquarters of the merchants, skilled craftsmen and money lenders, all of whom were primarily engaged in supplying goods or services to landlords. Whether he dealt with continental or native craftsmen and merchants did not matter to the lord. At his convenience he was patron of both. As his need to spend his revenue frequently preceded his seasonal rent days, he would borrow, equally indiscriminately, from those able to mobilise money for him: Jews, merchant-financiers or anyone else. The king was the most inveterate borrower of all. Landlords and king, then, had everyday relationships with the men of the towns —merchants, craftsmen, moneylenders. To the towns under their lordship they gradually sold privileges, privileges which gave townsmen some measure of independence from royal or seignorial officials. How far did these privileges enable a moneyed interest to come into being, independent of, or opposed to, landlordism? In a later period it was common to contrast the debt-ridden feudal spendthrift with the prudent bourgeois. Was there any tendency, in the boom period of demesne farming, for power to pass from feudal landlords to a rising merchant class? Was this the reason why, towards the end of the thirteenth century, town communities and merchant assemblies were beginning to enter, at the king's will, into the affairs of the realm?

Because of the diversity of geography, because of the regional character of rural life, because different towns had different lords, every town had its own peculiar commercial and institutional history. Yet some general statements can be made about urban history, just as they can about rural history; especially if the changing character of landlord-peasant society is kept in mind.

The fair prospect of acquiring little privileges was opening out before the men of the larger English towns in the earlier twelfth century. The dislocation and setbacks in town life incidental to the Norman Conquest were past history. Marcher lords were establishing new towns in the west; the older cities and larger boroughs were losing their semi-agricultural character, as they became the home of new groups of craftsmen and merchants, some of whom came from continental towns or villages, some from the English countryside. Peasants with only rural experience of carpentry, stone cutting, smithing, weaving, leather working, might well expect to maintain themselves in a town as full time workers; still more, craftsmen with a higher degree of skill in the making of cloth, armour, various leather goods, pottery, silver ware, indeed of any goods required by ecclesiastical and seignorial establishments. This concentration of certain types of industry in cities and boroughs well situated for trade, had begun, as we have seen, long before the twelfth century, both in Europe and in England; but it is an undocumented process whose social consequences were worked out gradually over a number of generations. Urban industry supplemented rather than supplanted village industry; its increasing specialisation, and the acquisition of higher degrees of skill are obvious facts, reflected in the elaboration of war equipment, the finer style of life in monastery and castle during the twelfth and thirteenth century. The continued progress of town life in England however was dependent on whether or not residents in English towns could organize their markets so as to obtain a share, if possible a major share, in the trade of supplying goods to landlords.

Each town had competitors. So far as is known the townsmen of the twelfth century had no economic theory of the legitimate function of foreign trade, no desire to exclude aliens as such from their town markets. On the contrary, there was a longstanding practice of international commerce. The import of wine or spices for example in no way cut across the interests of native merchants, as we will call the merchants resident in English towns, however cosmopolitan their background, in contra-distinction to the aliens, or merchants from continental towns. If, however, the native merchants had been numerous and wealthy enough, they would have confined the aliens to wholesale trading, buying from them for retail sale in their own town markets. Many native craftsmen needed imported raw materials; the cordwainers of London for example worked on Spanish leather; metal workers needed metals drawn from districts which lay far apart from each other; dyers needed alum, indigo, and other foreign dye stuffs. A characteristic trading group in a leading borough or city of twelfth century England would include some scores of independent craftsmen with their various skills; butchers, bakers and fishmongers supplying food to fellow townsmen; dealers in local food stuffs and the local raw materials of industry; and a few traders who regularly visited fairs outside the town area both to buy and sell. The craftsmen were independent in so far as they bought their own materials, owned their own tools, rented their own shops, and sold the articles they produced with their assistants, the apprentices and journeymen, as they were later called. It was still comparatively easy, at this stage of development, to adjust conflicting interests within such a group; in fact each was necessary to the other. It was politic to preserve the traditional principles of fair dealing and mutual support learnt on the great trade routes. Hence the formation of urban trading associations.

Obviously one of the first needs of a nascent community of traders was control of their local market as against the officials of the lord of the town, who was the king himself in many important cities and boroughs. In the most common form of undifferentiated trading association, the merchant guild, all who wished to trade in the town might be included on payment of fees into the common fund: aliens and men from neighbouring towns and villages, as well as the victuallers, craftsmen and merchants resident within the town walls. In London however, bakers, fishmongers, weavers, formed separate guilds, which took the place of earlier more primitive associations; and the Commune of London, when recognized in 1191, was already oligarchic. Kings were willing, in the twelfth century, to bargain with organised groups of burghers seeking recognition of their trading associations and borough customs. In piecemeal fashion liberties or privileges were granted for cash premiums. Given the fact that this was the time when the king and other magnates were willing to farm out manors to villagers for money rents, it would have been strange indeed if they had not farmed out their more important boroughs to a responsible group of burghers, better able to collect rents than their own officials. Only a few monastic houses thought their interest lay in keeping their burghers in an unprivileged condition. Merchant guilds, where they existed, were, then, normally recognised; henceforward, free from royal or seignorial interference, they collected stallage and tolls from traders who did not belong to the guild; with their common funds they protected their members in trading disputes or other difficulties, and paid contributions to sums due to the lord. They took action against traders who neglected the standard measures or infringed the trading regulations. In short the leading merchants of the town, through the guild, had a means of shaping a town policy; and as they met the rising competition of alien merchants, far more wealthy, better organized and numerous than they, they used the guild to exclude them from the town market. And in towns where there were many weavers or fullers or other numerous groups of craftsmen of the same trade, the merchants used the guild to regulate conditions of work to the benefit of the dominant merchants.

The fair prospects of the twelfth century did not entirely materialise in the second half of the twelfth century and early thirteenth century. The rapid development of industry and merchant capitalism in Flemish and Italian towns, tipped the balance unfavourably against the English towns. The prosperity of the latter increased, but only to a petty bourgeois level. The number of highly privileged alien merchants trading in England rapidly increased as continental industry developed. Not only did they divert, through their trade, raw materials from English towns to continental towns, they imported in bulk cloth and other commodities which English craftsmen might well have produced. The alliance of the big landlords with the aliens was a very formidable one. It worked in two ways, both to the detriment of the towns. First, contracts for bulk purchases of wool were made between aliens and the big woolgrowers as we have shown; these cut out the activities of merchant middlemen who would have sold some of the wool to native craftsmen. Second, the enormous increase in the number of fairs (and the lord of the fair pocketed the profits) diverted trade from the towns, and afforded facilities to aliens for selling their imports directly to seigniorial or royal officials and buying what they would for export. Even the privileges of the men of London or Winchester were superseded during the duration of a fair near their respective cities. In short, fairs helped the alien merchants to establish a stranglehold over the carrying trade between England and the continent. Alien merchants had also permanent trading stations in London and some other important towns. And it became common for them to make partnerships with native merchants, so that the latter traded with their money for part profits. In particular, aliens interested in the export of wool, used merchants from towns in wool growing districts to buy up wool for them from the villages near the town. In vain merchant guilds forbad their members to make contracts of this kind and threatened them with suspension or expulsion. They rightly judged that there was no more effective way of acting against the interests of the community of the town; but in the difficult trading position of the thirteenth century there was no better way for a local merchant to become rich. The few who were successful in the business of being junior partners to alien wool exporters usually transferred their headquarters to one of the great ports of Eastern England, in particular to London.

In London the number of the native wool exporters, about 1300, exceeded the number of aliens. In other ports, however, they were in a small minority. Wherever they dwelt their activities were inimical to the interests of the rank and file of small merchants in the English towns, especially after Edward I's decisive intervention in trade through the imposition of new and heavy customs duties.* His negotiations now with the small circle of rich native wool exporters, now with alien merchants, precipitated a major political struggle. The landlords and the general body of native merchants temporarily found themselves in mutual alliance against the king, the wool exporters, and alien importers. The former, as one would expect, resisted the efforts of the latter to pass their customs on in the shape of lower prices for wool or higher prices for imports. The subsequent running conflict continued into the mid-fourteenth century, by which time a new adjustment of interests had become possible.

This conflict, so closely linked with the formation of Parliament, as Eileen Power has shown, should remind us that towns in England did not achieve rights of self government which made them independent of the crown. For kings were building up a centralized government which threatened to make them absolute monarchs; from this there was no escape. Kings could confiscate charters and increase the annual farm rents taken from the burghers. In the twelfth century kings taxed their own cities and boroughs in much the same way as they taxed their demesne manors, by the arbitrary tallage. By the thirteenth century they had devised methods of taxing the liquid wealth of all the people of the realm; the men of cities and boroughs were obliged to contribute to these subsidies, when they were levied. Moreover in all the leading boroughs, the king's licensed money lenders, the Jews, were established. The profits which the Jews made by lending money at high interest to needy townsmen, peasants, gentry, clergy, monks and magnates, were

* E. Power, *The Wool Trade in English Medieval History*, pp. 63, seq.

appropriated by the crown, if not in their lifetime by tallages, at death, when their treasure and property passed into royal hands. By the end of the reign of Henry III the Jews had served their purpose; they were squeezed dry.. So Edward I drove them from the country, and turned to the firms of alien merchants and the native wool exporters when he wished to borrow money. As events showed, for a merchant to lend money to a powerful king was to risk ruin.

In this hostile commercial and financial environment, created partly by the great magnates' intervention both in production and in marketing, partly by the increasing power of the crown to tap the wealth of the trading classes through taxation, usury, and loans, it is not strange that the growth of English towns was relatively slow. Only London vied with the great towns of the continent in population, in the number and size of its crafts, and in the wide flung business of its merchants. Only in London did the conflict between the ruling oligarchy of merchants and victuallers, and the rising industrial crafts, end in a victory for the latter, who organised separate craft-guilds and secured a place in the governing body of the town. Elsewhere the crafts were not yet strong enough successfully to challenge the merchant dealers who were dominant in the affairs of the town. Although there were numerous small seignorial markets and fairs, there were relatively few privileged towns which had a population of over a thousand even in 1377, when the poll-tax records, which can be used as a basis for rough estimates of urban population, were made. And towns were finding it increasingly difficult, towards the end of the thirteenth century, to maintain the monopoly control of the regional market which seemed their only security. The formation of a class of English merchants with national as distinct from local or sectional interests had scarcely begun. The development of exchange in England had increased the wealth and freedom of the great magnates; it had facilitated the rise of a class of small landlords; it had contributed to the growth of Flemish and Italian industrial centres and had

made possible the meteoric rise of a few big merchant finan-
ciers most of whom, in England, were aliens, until the close
of the century. But it had retarded the development of
English industry and English merchant capital. The great
magnates and the crown still held the keys of the social
situation.

CHAPTER VII

LAW AND POLITICS, 1154-1307

IN 1154 when the reign of Henry II in England began, the
restoration of the order which had existed in the day of his
grandfather, Henry I, was proclaimed; but whether king or
magnates would take the lead in the inevitable political reconstruction was an open question. During the preceding
reign of Stephen, the liberties of the church had been extended without effective challenge, and some of the great
earls had pursued dynastic policies of their own. They had
sought to re-establish hereditary possession of local offices like
that of royal sheriff, constable and local justiciar; if logically
pursued this would have ended in the consolidation of a
few more or less autonomous and compact principalities
within the realm and reduced the area over which the crown
exercised direct control over its demesne lands, forests,
churches, shire courts, boroughs, and the rank and file of
the fee-holding class, the small tenants-in-chief and the
under tenants. The small unitary feudal principality was
easier to build up than a feudal kingdom within which a
complex balance of baronial, royal and ecclesiastical rights
and liberties had to be maintained. On the other hand the
need for a more flexible, effective and rational law, latent
in all groups of the feudal class, afforded an opportunity
for the unification of the realm of which Henry II made
good use. When he died in 1189 the possibility that the realm

of England would be reconstructed as a federation of small feudal states no longer existed. The shires were firmly under the control of royal sheriffs who held their office on a temporary basis; within them the small landlords perforce accepted the new duties which the king's government thrust upon them. The king's court was still itinerant; but at Westminster, where it often rested, there was a permanent department of state, the Exchequer, where royal officials skilled in financial and judicial work were beginning to keep elaborate records and to understand the way in which the common law of the realm could be expanded and royal finance modernised. In the shires, sheriffs closely controlled by Westminster were increasingly occupied with implementing the hundreds of writs which came from Exchequer or Chancery, bidding them collect particular debts or empanel juries; almost every year, justices from Westminster came to "take the assises"; at longer intervals they carried out wholesale stocktaking on behalf of the king. In short the realm was a single administrative unit. A bureaucracy was rapidly expanding its activities; all groups in the *feudal* class, according to their social standing, were co-operating in its work, although the magnates still formed an inner circle without whose collaboration the king would be unable to act effectively. The purpose of this chapter is to consider how this centralisation of the state took place, what functions it served, what tensions it caused, and how far these tensions were counteracted, before the class position of the great magnates was challenged by the economic crisis of the fourteenth century.

I

In 1154 king Henry II and most of his prelates and earls and barons had interests outside England. Henry II was ruler not only of the Norman conquests in England and the Anglo-Norman conquests in Wales and eventually in Ireland, but of a vast and unstable complex of territories in Western France, centring on the Loire, but including both Aquitaine and Normandy; for these he owed homage to the King of France. Among his barons in England were men belonging to families who had a wide network of fees in France and men engrossed in the possibilities of expansion into the Celtic lands of Wales and Ireland. There were also bishops or abbots, who might, in a crisis, put their loyalties to the Church before their obligations to the king. He moved restlessly from one centre of his scattered dominions to another; to maintain and develop his territorial rights meant ceaseless political effort, even apart from counteracting the intrigues of his sons, his barons or his bishops. The respect for strict legality, already implicit in feudal custom, proved an indispensable weapon in his diplomacy.

Within England as within the French fiefs there was a close connection between the growth of centralized political institutions and governmental technique, and the economic and social development which we have sketched in the last chapter. For example, the problems met by the common law largely arose from the continuous piecemeal redistribution of land; the problems of the financial administration, from the new opportunities of making higher profits out of old rights. The changing economic environment of Christendom however, although decisive, was not the only dynamic factor in political development. The reform movement in the Church and the renaissance of legal studies, indeed the whole intellectual movement which centred in the cathedral schools and the universities of Paris and Bologna, were also vital in and after 1154. They help to account for the shift of political emphasis from military expansion to fiscal exploitation, the strong tendency towards the centralisation of government both in Church and state, the emergence of a professional civil-servant approach to the problems of law and administration, and the growth of political propaganda. These developments were part of the process of reconstruction proceeding within Christendom.

Reconstruction was first achieved within the Church; so it affected the development of all the constituent units of

Western Christendom. In its attempt to solve the problem of protecting its land and immunities, the Church transformed itself, in the course of the twelfth century from a federation of local churches into a closely knit institution directed by a Pope who claimed jurisdiction over kings as well as the clerical hierarchy. To his court came appeals from every part of Europe. Meanwhile monasteries ceased to be the chief educational centres of Christendom as learned clerks, and later, new orders of friars, took up the problems of their day and so influenced, as we have suggested, the practical approach to politics both of ecclesiastical and lay rulers. In this movement there were two well defined phases, the second fulfilling the first.

The reform movement started as a succession of rather spasmodic efforts to improve the discipline of the clergy in accordance with the better traditions of the church. It came under the direction of the Papacy in 1048. Hildebrand, as Gregory VII, tried to force the pace (1073-1084). In his time the reform movement became profoundly disturbing, a menace and a challenge to lay rulers; but it was still rooted in the traditions of the early Papacy. Any cleric would have thought like Hildebrand if, like that Pope, he had mentally underlined passages about Papal power in an important text book of canon law known to us as the Pseudo-Isidore. This had been compiled in the Carolingian period. In the eleventh century it was difficult to detect the forgeries of a previous age, even of obvious fabrications like the Donation of Constantine, which purported to delegate imperial authority in the West to the Papacy. In Hildebrand's mind the canonical conception of Papal power was given greater moral force by the traditional theological conception of justice. Society was only rightly organised when the essential superiority of priests and of the law of the Church was recognised and made implicit in the political order; for the Pope, "the successor of St. Peter and the vicar of Christ," rather than kings, should control the bishops of a realm and compel them to enforce the canon law against the bad customs which kings had formerly fostered. Kings, like bishops, should be compelled by ecclesiastical sentences of excommunication to co-operate in this work of enforcing valid law; or else they too could be deposed, like mere bailiffs. In other words the iniquity against which Hildebrand declared war was embodied in those customs which had grown up in Germany and England and smaller feudal states through the close political alliance of princes and bishops, customs which undoubtedly tended to introduce *feudal* principles into the tenure of ecclesiastical offices and consequently to make the maintenance of clerical discipline difficult. Simony, or the giving and acceptance of cash premiums for ecclesiastical benefices, lay investiture, the marriage of clergy were, so it was thought, at the root of the evil. No one however took seriously a suggestion, made by a later pope in the course of the controversy, of solving this problem of Church discipline by a partial disendowment of the Church—the taking back of benefices given to the Church for secular services. The influence and the independence of the Church was, so it was thought, bound up with its control of landed estates; and there is little doubt that the judgment was correct.

The Hildebrandine programme was not as yet practical politics. There were few bishops who were prepared to obey papal decrees aimed at customs which, as they thought, worked well enough. No king in his senses would allow his kingdom to be disrupted by giving up control over the personnel of his episcopate. In Germany, the programme fomented an existing conflict between the Emperor and the magnates for two generations. Even in England, where there was an overriding need for unity between the Norman conquerors, it acted as a stimulus to a reform of the Church by the king. William the Conqueror, evidently calculating that a king was never more a king than when he was a theocrat, as kings like Charlemagne and Alfred had been, authorised his archbishop, Lanfranc, to carry out such ecclesiastical reforms as did not interfere with royal rights. Thus, although bishops were encouraged to study and apply the canon law in their own courts by the archbishop, they were still appointed by the king, and were compelled to render *feudal* service for their bishoprics. The king acted as intermediary between the Papacy and the Church in England; he could for example prevent the publication of papal decrees in his realm. A canon of York, who drafted some of the many pamphlets produced during the Investitures Contest, worked out an uncompromising defence of the theocratic conception of kingship.

Meanwhile the Church was educating a new generation of young men, able and willing to undertake administrative work for kings or to pursue a career in the Church. If the Hildebrandine programme had stimulated study of the canon law, criticism of it quickened interest in the classical Roman law, study of which had already begun at Pavia and Bologna. Such studies, early in the twelfth century, could be undertaken not only in some of the Italian towns, where the educational system of the late Roman Empire had never entirely withered away, but also in the schools of the churches of the West, especially those of Northern France; and later of England. As Latin was the only medium for lectures and discussion, students could move freely to any scholastic centre to which they were drawn by the fame of a particular teacher. After mastering the elements of grammar, logic and rhetoric, an intellectual *élite* proceeded to the study of law or theology according to the kind of career which they had in mind. All these were studies uncoloured by any provincial traditions. The assimilation of texts inherited from the Roman Empire and the Early Church; the adoption of some of the learning which trickled into Europe from the lands of Arabs or Greeks; the application of knowledge so acquired to the intellectual problems thrown up by the changing society of Western Christendom; these were the tasks on which students and teachers in the twelfth century exercised their wits and enthusiasm. One branch of study influenced another at this time, for specialised studies were in their infancy. So the study of canon law was influenced both by the study of Roman law and theology; theology in its turn by law and the new enthusiasm for Aristotelian logic. The student of the liberal arts, if he had ability, had the kind of all-round learning which would enable him to toss off a love song or a satiric poem, write a semi-philosophical treatise or history, draft a letter or a political pamphlet or a charter, as need arose. The scholar was more often a man of affairs than a recluse. Meanwhile sustained study and discussion in the schools were leading to further assimilation of legal and philosophical materials; and the thirteenth century consequently was the age of the great scholastic systematisation of medieval knowledge.

The twelfth-century legal renaissance reacted quickly on ecclesiastical organisation. Methods and principles originally gained from study of Roman law, were applied to the urgent task of rationalising and digesting the often discordant sources for the law of the Church, which enthusiasts for the cause of Church reform had long been studying. So some of the general principles of canon law were clarified, and, more important, its inadequacies and vagueness about procedure revealed. This stage is conveniently marked by the compilation of the new text book, the Decretum, by a doctor of Bologna, Gratian, about 1140. Meanwhile young men who were influenced by this movement or who had even played a leading part in it, were climbing into key positions in the church, as archdeacons, bishops and Popes. From the mid-twelfth century the need for a law-making authority in the church was widely recognised both by canonists and by legal minded archdeacons and bishops attempting to apply the law of the church in their dioceses. And what better authority than a semi-imperial Pope could be found? The superior authority of Papal decrees over other sources of the law of the Church had already been worked out as a principle of criticism. From about 1140 started the common practice of transferring pleas which had arisen in local churches to the judgment of the Papal curia; the epoch making pontificate was that of Alexander III (1162-1180), the first of the great jurist popes.* Thenceforward judgments made in the Papal curia, or by judges appointed by the Pope, if important enough, could be incorporated into the common law of the Church. At first a supplement of the old law, these judgments became for practical purposes the actual canon law, applied in the dioceses and studied in the schools. Throughout the thirteenth century this more flexible and scientific law was being made. By a legal process which Hildebrand had not visualised, but which in retrospect he seemed to have set in motion, the Papacy became a source of order and equity for the Church in the West. In Maitland's phrase the Pope became the "Universal Ordinary".

Other kinds of business concentrated in the Papal curia, as if in fulfilment of the Hildebrandine ideal. For the Papacy, in this period, had the authority and initiative to capture and direct important movements within Christendom. It assumed, for example, leadership of the Crusading movement and consequently the power of taxing the incomes of ecclesiastics. In the thirteenth century it assumed powers of *providing* to cathedral prebends, parish churches, and, in certain cases, to bishoprics, so overriding the ordinary rights of patrons or electors. It took under its wing the nascent universities and the orders of friars. It set up special tribunals for the suppression of heresies. From time to time it summoned general councils of the church, and issued decrees of general application which were incorporated into the law of the church. Finally, to protect its temporal power in Italy, it intervened in politics and so became involved in a series of expensive wars, which impinged on the politics of the German Empire, of France, Spain and England. Among the states of Christendom only the kingdom of France was sovereign in the thirteenth century in the sense that its kings did not acknowledge the *feudal* overlordship of Popes, or, as in the case of the Empire, Papal superiority.

* G. Barraclough, *Papal Provisions*, pp. 2-3, and F. W. Maitland, *Canon Law in the Church of England*.

This decisive reorientation of the ecclesiastical system, behind which was a continuous and constructive intellectual
movement, helped to determine the development of the
centralized state in England. For kings, no less than popes
and bishops, could be served by learned clerks. Kings could
meet the challenge of the Church, by building up the counter
jurisdiction of their own courts, in much the same way as
the jurisdiction of the Papal curia had been extended. In
conjunction with economic factors, the growth of the centralized Church made inevitable the integration of England
within an international system, for a time. But it in no way
impeded the processes which were making monarchy the
most powerful force within the state.

The centralization of government within the realm of
England through the growth of a common law, the law of
the king's court, was far more than a response to the challenge of the Church. Henry II's initial interest in this unit
of his dominions was not different in kind from the interest
of a lay baron in his private estate or honour. It was a
revenue-producing concern, the source of the wealth which
enabled him to play his due part in Christendom. It was a
complex of profitable rights: manorial rights; judicial and
fiscal rights which could be described as regalian rights; and
feudal rights, the reserve rights over the fees granted to
tenants. If exploitation of purely manorial rights on the
part of a great magnate was best effected through a methodical written record of rights and dues, by a constant shift of
emphasis from one set of rights to another as new expedients
for raising money became possible, by the creation of a
hierarchy of officials to prevent local agents from lining their
pockets with profits claimed by the lord, (and this, as we have
seen, was what feudal lords achieved) how much more was
it expedient for the crown to proceed by similar methods in
the exploitation of its wider range of profitable rights?
Henry I had already made a beginning along such lines;

Henry II could begin his reconstruction by saying he was restoring the customs of his grandfather.

Manorial rights stood outside law and politics. Just as it was no concern of the king how his feudal tenants dealt with the peasants on their estates, so the administration of the royal demesne manors was not a matter of public interest. In the view of the justices, as we shall call the royal officials who did judicial work for the crown, peasants were serfs, men subject to the will of the lord. This we have already emphasised. In the exploitation of their regalian and *feudal* rights, however, kings had to act with the advice of their magnates and to observe the customs of the realm. Such was the long-standing tradition. Henry II was as keenly interested in juristic ideas as any of the great popes or school-men of the age; he enjoyed discussion with the learned clerks who were among the men whom he used for managing his various affairs. So far as judicial business was concerned, however, there was no question of adopting Roman law to form the basis of a common law. Just as the common law of the Church was built up on the basis of its own tradition, so in England the king and his justices worked from the unwritten, largely archaic customs of the shire courts, and the customary *feudal* law of the honour courts and the king's court, which had developed during the previous century. General principles became implicit in practice, as the king's court devised new procedures to deal with the kind of cases which were most frequently brought to its notice with a plea for redress. It became a principle, for example, that any free-holder, whoever was his lord, could seek royal justice if he was evicted from a tenement "unlawfully and without a judgment", or if he was unable to obtain possession of what he claimed as his inheritance. It became a principle that, if a man wished to avoid the barbarous hazards of the duel in defending his right to any fragment of his estate, he could apply to the king for a writ setting in motion an action in which the issue turned on the verdict of a jury. No free-holder need answer for his land unless the man who claimed it from him obtained the king's writ. The details of these new actions devised by the king, sometimes after sleepless nights and laborious days of discussion, are not in themselves important. They were however practical and efficient enough to attract a vast amount of business to the king's court. The king's justices established a monopoly over them, so that, as their numbers and scope increased during the thirteenth century, the archaic customs of the shire courts were forgotten and the civil business left to the honour courts* dwindled to a few formalities. The jurisdiction of the ecclesiastical courts, which had expanded so rapidly in the first half of the twelfth century, was restricted and even encroached upon in the thirteenth century. The king's court normally dealt with disputes about churches and church fees and pleas in which a breach of faith was concerned, in spite of initial claims by the Church for this vast field of jurisdiction.

The king's court organised its justice so that both the revenue and authority of the crown was increased. Writs and concords were paid for. Justices were sent on tour round the shires to deal with the various new actions or assizes, or, if the litigants preferred, they were brought before the king's justices at Westminster, now the centre of the administrative system of the realm. In either case they consulted a jury empanelled from freeholders or knights of the neighbourhood where the dispute had arisen; questions were put to these juries which bore upon the crucial matter of fact. On their sworn answers or verdicts the issue turned. If the case was complicated however, or if it directly concerned the king or very powerful men, or if there had been an alleged miscarriage of justice, the matter could be brought before the king himself, and determined by the king and his council. It was this practice which, during the mid-thirteenth century, produced a quickening flow of various kinds of petitions to the king and the development of legal discussion between

* See Denholm-Young, *Seignorial Administration in England*, pp. 86-99.

the king in Council, common law judges and the leading officials of the Exchequer. No single factor was more important in the first stage of the growth of Parliament.*

The territorial interests of the great landlords and gentry were safeguarded rather than challenged by the common law. They were the men who took their pleas to the king's court. Undoubtedly the royal judges helped manorial lords of different social standing to vindicate their rights as against each other. Although the business of the honour courts declined, the great barons were left with control over their customary tenants, the suitors of their manor courts, and a wide measure of control over their franchises. They were given new means of recovering runaway serfs or dealing with serfs who claimed to be free of labour services or immune from an increase in these services. In the thirteenth century too a procedure by which bailiffs were forced to render account was created. Moreover the better keeping of the peace which Henry II inaugurated† was greatly to the advantage of all who were interested in manorial profits and peaceful trade. Crimes like murder, highway robbery, cattle theft, arson, false coinage, not only impeded agriculture and trade, they fostered among the villagers "a spirit of unrest and insubordination". To deal with lawless men on a local basis was ineffective. On the whole then the barons were prepared to consent to the centralisation of traditional police measures and to allow the king to collect the profits of high criminal justice, even although this meant that they lost the profits

---

* The word only meant parley; royal parliaments at this stage were, sometimes between the council and different state departments, sometimes between the king and his magnates, etc. No one in the mid-thirteenth century could forsee that a "house of commons" would one day form the most important element in an institution which had sovereign power. See F. M. Powicke, *Henry III and Lord Edward*, Vol. I, p. 338-41.

† Royal justices were sent to the shire courts to hear the indictments of criminals made by jurors from the villages and hundreds, and to conduct the trials of suspect criminals whom the sheriff had taken in charge.

of their own rights of jurisdiction over thieves. True, the police system was only partially effective; sometimes men were driven to the woods to escape the savagery of justice and peasants connived with outlaws and refused to indict their friends. So an undercurrent of violence persisted in English life even during the most peaceful phase of feudal development, augmented on occasions, by the turbulence of young knights attending tournaments and by the affrays of their armed retainers. The justices, often if not invariably, were mainly concerned with the financial aspect of their business. The peasants and townsmen, who were forced to bear the burden of the police system, were *amerced* for the least fault. "It was almost impossible for a man however much he might try to do his duty to escape amercement".* Incidentally the knights and freeholders who acted as jurors in civil pleas were also liable to amercement. The justices when they came into the shires inspired a dread; they were not, in their time, regarded as champions of the 'common man'.

The king's justices did not only tour the shires to hear common pleas, to supervise the police system, and to deliver the gaols. They were concerned with the whole range of the king's rights, manorial, regalian and *feudal,* and the conduct of local government. Men from the countryside were called upon to make sworn verdicts in many administrative enquiries. The justices as fiscal agents of the crown thus formed a link between the sheriffs and other local officials, and the Exchequer, the department of the king's court which collected the royal revenues and implemented new expedients for augmenting them; and also served as the head-quarters of the justices. They were not the only link. From the time of Henry I the sheriffs accounted twice yearly at the Exchequer, for the farm rent of the shire and other sums due from men of the shire to the king which they had been ordered to collect. A London chronicler in the time of Henry

---

* A. Lane-Poole, *Obligations of Society in the XII and XIII Centuries.* p. 81. The whole chapter on amercements, or fines, is important.

I said that the sheriffs shook with terror as they assembled to render their accounts; for the purpose of the audit was to detect ways in which they were making illicit profits out of their office. As the king's fiscal system became more complex and efficient the sheriff's tasks were considerably modified. In the thirteenth century other officials were made responsible for collecting and accounting for the principal regular items of the king's revenue, including the income from manors and escheats, the income from the forests, and from the customs. The sheriff's main fiscal job in this period was to collect debts due to the crown. But the Exchequer remained as the centralising authority, exerting a relentless pressure on the hierarchy of local officials and through them on all classes of the king's subjects.

It was in practice very difficult to draw the line between ordinary authorised oppression and arbitrary oppression in collecting sums due to the king. Underlings of the sheriff for example had the power of seizing a debtor's chattels, including his flocks and herds and plough animals, and then selling them, if the debtor could not otherwise pay. This was a practice which afforded loopholes for bribery, extortion, violence, petty malice; all the evils endemic to the system, which the king's justices, to give them their due, sometimes made efforts to eradicate. In fact they could no more prevent dishonesty or petty tyranny on the part of local officials, than civil service chiefs to-day could prevent petty rudeness in their local offices. The victims of unauthorised oppression were usually small men; although probably the local gentry as well as the peasantry enjoyed the ballads which told their tales of how bad sheriffs were outwitted by outlaws. Already in the thirteenth century the peasants were articulating grievances in bad verse: grievances for example against bailiffs who collected the same debt more than once:

"The bedels they hunt us as hounds hunt the hare,
  For they escape unpunished and we are always caught".*

* For abuses in local government, see H. M. Cam, *The Hundred and the Hundred Rolls*, (London, 1930).

If the royal fiscal system pressed upon everyone, from serf to magnate, it pressed most harshly on the men who were near the borderline of poverty—the villagers who could be intimidated and beaten up with impunity. And in their experience the oppression of baronial officials in the franchises and the oppression of the king's sheriffs and bailiffs in the shires and royal hundreds were two aspects of the same system.

III

The tenants-in-chief of the crown came directly and frequently into contact with the king's fiscal system. A few examples will illustrate the character of such contacts. Lay baronies, if the heir was a minor, and bishoprics, during vacancies, were administered by crown officials; often they were restored in a shamefully impoverished condition. Before 1215 the crown could exact what sum it could from the heir of an earl or baron as a relief. Scutages, which before 1215 were levied at the discretion of the crown, were collected almost yearly by King John. The more occasional taxes on moveables, which were collected by special royal commissions, fell upon all propertied classes. As this was a new method of raising an aid, and a means for the crown to appropriate a share of the profits of trade and wool and corn production, no levy could be collected without causing bad feeling. It is true however that levies were infrequent and that magnates could recoup themselves in part by raising a tallage from the unfree tenants of their demesne manors, just as, in the case of scutage, they collected the necessary sum from their tenants by knight service. Taxation was annoying rather than ruinous for the magnates. Probably it was less annoying than the Exchequer's remorseless challenges of the validity of their rights to profit by particular franchises;* these became frequent in and after the third decade of the thirteenth centuries. Fiscal grievances contributed very largely

---

* For illustrations of the expenses of the consequent litigation, see Denholm-Young, *Seignorial Administration in England*, pp. 111-116.

to the determination of the magnates to control, in their own
interests, the working of the royal bureaucracy. They were
not however the immediate cause of the crucial quarrels
which from time to time split the ruling class, ranging
'opposition' barons against barons who supported the crown,
during the period 1213-1267.

Before considering these conflicts, it is important to realise
that the royal officials were not a class or group set apart
from the baronage. Only a few of the court officials came from
lands outside England. The majority were drawn from the
lower stratum of the manor-holding class. Such men were
not the social equals of earls and great barons; but the
relationship was like that of colonel and lieutenant, not
master and man. No magnate who was proud of his ancestry
could take it as a matter of course when a court official,
through the king's patronage and cash down, secured the
marriage of a noble heiress or received an escheated barony.
Yet such things happened. Successful service in the king's
court was normally accompanied by social promotion. Many
of the great barons of the thirteenth century had ancestors
who had been "raised from the dust" by Henry I or one of
the Angevin kings. Similarly, successful clerks might hope,
by the king's good will and influence, to become bishops;
then, sometimes without giving up their official position at
court, they would rank among the most important of the
king's tenant-in-chief. Meanwhile the working of the king's
government was drawing the rank and file of the knights and
rich freeholders of the shires into the shire courts. As jurors,
as coroners, as hundred bailiffs, as sheriffs, escheators, fores-
tors etc., they gained experience of administration. Under
the eye of travelling justices they ran the shire courts, and
in the middle decades of the thirteenth century were frequently travelling to Westminster on the king's business.

The magnates, once they began to realise the potential
advantages of centralised government, (and the realisation
of its advantages ran parallel to experience of its dangers)
would not object to the gentry shouldering the burdens of

local government. Their sphere of political activity was the king's court. The duties which the gentry fulfilled in the shire courts at the king's command, weakened, but did not destroy, their pre-existing obligations to *feudal* lords. The same type of man who served the king, served as stewards or bailiffs of barons. Indeed in the thirteenth century the first beginnings of that system of livery and maintenance which developed fast in the period of declining feudalism can be detected. Until a man had climbed very high up the ladder of promotion offered by the court, he could not afford to antagonise a great magnate or a seignorial official of his home neighbourhood. Any local official, seignorial or royal, had powers of inflicting injuries.

So the gentry, the lower stratum of the *feudal* class, served both kings and magnates; gentry and lay magnates, king, court officials and prelates had interlocking interests. They were a ruling class, whose fundamental solidarity was troubled and disturbed by only superficial tensions and con-flicting interests; if the brittle peace were broken no simple horizontal or vertical cleavages would follow. In theory the mutual rights and obligations of the various groups within the *feudal* class were well recognised; for example it was in the interests of both the magnates and the crown to be aware of the grievances of the shire gentry and to promise redress, especially in times of crisis. A baronial struggle for control of the royal bereaucracy, would, by the constitution of the *feudal* class, become inseparable from a struggle to lead the shire gentry. Even in 1215 the magnates who drew up the great Charter of Liberties could not dis-regard the interests of the small landlords.

The baronial struggle to control the king's administration and to maintain their position as advisors of the crown gathered force during the thirteenth century. It kept pace with an increasingly bitter fear that the king might dispense with their co-operation with serious consequences to their own security. Particular episodes gave substance to this fear. Aided by his officials King John defied the papacy for several years, which meant that he ruled without some of his most important advisers, the bishops, whose estates meanwhile were administered by and for, the crown. Then came the years of 'tyranny' in 1213-1215 in which few barons felt safe. In 1233-1234, the whole court administration and nearly every office whose profits were paid into the exchequer, was concentrated in the hands of a single court official, Peter des Rivaux. Henry III took counsel only of Peter des Roches, the bishop of Winchester, a former court official of King John. The dark days of King John seemed to have returned. How could a magnate be sure of justice in such a situation? Even so great a man as Hubert de Burgh, with his wide network of lordships (Hubert de Burgh is an example of a man of no great family who rose to high baronial rank in the king's service) had been imprisoned and dispossessed without trial. Richard Marshall, Earl of Pembroke, so it was rumoured, was treacherously murdered, by order of the court. And the king had landed mercenary soldiers from the continent to subdue the righteous resistance of his own barons! These were extreme examples of what a king might do if he escaped from the feudal control of his barons, lay and ecclesiastical. In general the thirteenth-century baronage thought that unless they continued their traditional collaboration with the crown in the great council, unless the king had one or two permanent baronial councillors, the king's patronage would pass them by in favour of upstart officials or needy royal relatives; the king would press his financial claims against them with impunity and waste their resources and his own, on schemes from which they derived no benefit. The fabric of centralised government was too useful for them to contemplate tearing it down. The common law, if it was well observed, would protect their rights and those of the gentry, as well as the legitimate rights of the crown. If it was not observed, kingship would become tyranny.

In the crisis of King John's reign, the opposition barons did not begin by waging war against the crown; they looked for a way of protecting the liberties of the whole *feudal* class by a statement of common law which the court administration would accept as the law of the land. This was the famous Charter of Liberties; it was not a reactionary document; it was a careful and very comprehensive statement of how the king's government should be run. On the whole it was based upon the practice of the later twelfth century; but various administrative reforms were suggested. Not all of them were accepted by the baronial government which functioned during the minority of Henry III (1216-1227); but in this vital period a revised Charter of Liberties became the criterion of good government.

When in a later age English politicians and historians began to think how the English Constitution with its limited monarchy and sovereign Parliament came into being, they pictured the thirteenth-century barons, who in fact defended feudalism, as the first Whigs. The Charter of Liberties started a tradition which was consummated in the Bill of Rights. Edmund Burke, for example, in his polemic against the levelling tendencies of the French Revolution, violently affirmed this theory of continuity. For the Tory historian, Bishop Stubbs, that doubtful character, Earl Simon de Montfort, that "buccaneering old Gladstone", was redeemed in so far as he had been one of the first to see "the uses and glories" of parliamentary institutions. Even more recently Simon de Montfort has been portrayed as a revolutionary radical; the reforms of the barons in 1258-60 have been treated as the "first revolution in English History". "If their project was not a revolution, our history has known none yet".* From the point of view of understanding what the barons really wanted in 1258 such analogies are, to say the least, misleading. In the thirteenth century there was no possibility of power passing from class to class, which is what happens in revolutions; there was not even a possibility of eliminating the king, or the baronage, or the gentry, from public life. Feudalism was at its zenith, not nearing its end;

* R. F. Treharne, *The Significance of the Baronial Reform Movement,* 1258-1267 in T.R.H.S., 1943.

and a struggle within the ruling class might still be resolved by an improvement in its constitution.

The barons who tried to reform the king's government during the years 1258-1260 by themselves controlling and directing the royal bureaucracy, were neither conservatives nor revolutionaries. They were feudalists moving confidently within the narrow circle of the ideas and political practice of their time. Theirs was a zeal for reform which sprang from contemporary confidence in the essential rightness and permanence of the social order in which they lived. In that legalistic age it was easy to cherish the illusion that divergencies of interest within a class could be adjusted by compromise and definition. Reform meant simply the elimination of certain bad customs; and to whip up enthusiasm for a plan to wipe these out of the system of royal government was easy enough, seeing that every group and class in society suffered from them. To justify themselves and to secure the support of the gentry, the baronage promised to reform their own administration of their courts and franchises. The maxim that the king ought to do justice and abide by the law was century old; the whole tradition of *feudalism*, as well as the way in which the common law had recently developed, gave confidence that the baronage were the body who could bind the king to his obligations. Ideas which were once the exclusive property of the clergy were now through sermons and popular poems reaching the unlettered and mixing in their minds with popular legends. A bishop, Robert Grosseteste, could hand on to a magnate, Simon de Montfort, a treatise on tyrannicide. Bishops who had faced the wrath of kings were accounted saints: Hugh of Lincoln, Edmund of Abingdon, Richard Wych. After his death Simon de Montfort was regarded by the people more as a martyr saint than as a baron who had plunged deep into the risks of court politics.

It is probable that the king in 1258 took the oath to abide by a baronial plan of reform as an expeditious way of evading the financial consequences of his unwise foreign policy. With disciplined eagerness the barons seized their opportunity of showing that they could govern better than the king. Justice need not be accompanied by extortion; all wrongs could be righted; the king could live of his own, after his debts were cleared. They drew up a plan of reform by which committees of barons acting in Council and in three annual parliaments, should, with the help of the departments of state, over which baronial officials were placed, amend the law, provide remedies for the grievances of holders of small fees, and control the various administrative departments. In every shire committees of knights were to be chosen to enquire into local grievances, in preparation for the arrival of the newly appointed justiciar; all, rich or poor, by simply making a complaint against an oppressive official, would get justice. As the baronial government set about its various tasks, it became clear that it intended to give the shire gentry a recognized if subordinate place in the new order. The sheriffdom was to be held by native knights of the shires, chosen by committees of gentry from their own members, not nominated by the Exchequer. Knights were summoned to Westminster in 1258; in 1259 in the shires a standing committee of four knights were to keep watch on the doings of the sheriff, to advise him to emend any of his misdeeds or, if he did not, report them to the central government. The conception of the shire as a community in which the gentry and freeholders were to act as a check on arbitrary local administration, while the greater baronage directed the central courts, was implicit in these provisions. Very clearly, through positive administrative achievements, the barons put across their claim to lead the shire gentry and protect the men of the shires against the tyranny of officialdom. Although there was no attempt to encroach upon royal rights, the plan was to control the king's use of them and to take from him the initiative in choosing his councillors and his officials and perhaps of disposing of his patronage. It was as if he were a minor or an imbecile.

Here was the most obvious weakness in the plan. The king was in his senses and by skilful diplomacy he won powerful support in Europe against this baronial attempt to place limitations on his freedom of action. The Papacy rejected the eloquent plea of the barons for its support of their venture. It absolved the king from his oath to observe the baronial provisions, so giving him "the free use in all things of the plenitude of royal power". The king of France and the Savoyard relatives of the king gave their moral or material support, as they could. Troops could be and were raised in France to fight for the king's liberty in England. Meanwhile the baronial government was losing its efficiency and its unity. Enthusiasm for administrative work and legal reforms was at a low ebb. It was easy enough for Henry III to succeed in the first stages of his struggle to regain the initiative. By 1261 he had re-established control over his council and the chief offices and suspended the judicial proceedings in the shires. It was less easy to follow this up by restoring disciplined subservience in the shires. There, initial baronial efficiency in the judicial proceedings and work of legal reform had made a good impression; the provision that sheriffs should be chosen from the shire gentry had been popular. The royalist sheriffs, appointed by Henry III in 1261, were not trusted; they were not local men. In sixteen shires the gentry placed their own men as wardens to oppose the royal sheriffs and collect the royal dues. This movement of rebellion was fostered by those few barons who had not made their peace with the king. In April 1263, at their invitation, Simon de Montfort, the most uncompromising and sincere of the barons who had played a leading part in the attempted reform of 1258-1260, reappeared in the country to start again the fight for the reform plan. This was the signal for a new wave of rebellion.

Simon de Montfort's partisans, who in certain shires included many of the clergy and large numbers of unimportant freeholders, attacked and plundered and appropriated the manors of royalists. Old grudges were scored off without waiting for the slow processes of the law. Meanwhile the Welsh prince, Llywelyn ap Gruffydd, who had built up a unified lordship over free Wales, was capturing royalist strongholds in the Marches. In London there was a civic revolution; the men of the rising crafts successfully challenged the merchant oligarchy which had held power up to 1263; the support of the city was given to Simon de Montfort; attacks were made on Jews and alien merchants and, according to the London chronicler, practically "the whole body of the middle folk of England" were aroused. A royalist chronicler said that in nearly every city and town respectable citizens were oppressed by "conspiracies of low fellows"; for in the towns, as in the country, 1263 gave a chance of settling old grievances or ambitions. Faced then with shire and borough communities seditiously seething with frustration and hope, Henry III gave way. Again he placed himself under the tutelage of the baronial provisions and Simon de Montfort. On Simon fell the hopeless task of restoring order and unity without seizing royal power or abandoning the reformist idealism of 1258.

Needless perhaps to say that he failed. "Protector of all the people of England", a baronial propagandist called him: * but even if Simon had been like the later Protector, society was not ready for a Cromwell. The clergy, the gentry, the townsmen, the barons, the men of the Marches were indeed divided; but only on how best to order the feudal state. There was no revolutionary situation; only the possibility of anarchy if the problem was not resolved. For Simon himself and probably for the clergy, the gentry and the townsmen who supported him, if not the baronial hotheads and the free peasantry, the main question after 1263 was how to restore the mid-thirteenth century conditions of feudal stability and legality. The effort to do this merely gave opportunities to the royalists to reopen the struggle for power. Hence the fine feudal heroics of the battle of Lewes, when Simon de Montfort and his partisans fought and beat the king (1264). Supported as the royalists were by powerful forces outside England, including the Papacy, their

* *Political Songs,* ed. Wright (Camden Series, R.H.S.), p. 124.

victory was only a matter of time. The battle of Evesham was the royalist retort to Lewes (1265). Simon de Montfort was killed; royalists vindictively turned upon the baronial partisans, seizing their lordships before the legal orders of forfeiture were issued. Masses of under-tenants were turned from their homes. So desperately the "disinherited" fought on. Bands of desperadoes roamed the countryside; until at last a compromise settlement on the territorial question was reached. Then at last the restoration of order in a temporarily impoverished countryside became possible. So the already rich popular traditions of resistance to authority were re-inforced. Precedents were established for both peasant and baronial revolts in the next two centuries. Precedents were also created for summoning knights and burgesses to West-minster when parliaments were being held. The task of amending the common law begun in 1258-9 was continued. The Statute of Marlborough confirmed enactments of these years (1267); an equilibrium only slightly different from that of tradition was restored. The theoretical statement of this equilibrium is perhaps best found in the words of an Edwardian lawyer, sometimes ascribed to the great lawyer Bracton who had been fully in sympathy with the baronial plan of 1258: "The king has a superior, namely God, as also the law, by which he is made king, and his court, that is the earls and barons . . . . And therefore if the king is unbridled, that is without law, they ought to put a bridle upon him, unless they, together with the king, are unbridled. And in that case the subject people will cry out and say 'Lord Jesus, with bit and bridle bind fast their jaws'."* This was a *feudal* social theory: none below the rank of earls and barons could take the political initiative.

IV

The reign of Edward (1272-1307) saw the zenith of monarchical power within the feudal state. Thanks to the

* Quoted by H. G. Richardson in *The Commons and Medieval Politics*, in T.R.H.S., 1946.

economic expansion, the magnates and gentry were able to concentrate on getting rich by efficient estate management. The activities of aliens and native merchants in overseas trade, as we have seen, had opened up a vast potential source of revenue for the crown. By increasing the traditional customs duties Edward I went a long way towards freeing the crown from its dependence on *feudal* taxation for carrying out large scale military operations. The English baronage however and the king had a common interest in reducing Wales to subjection and attempting to counteract the growing pressure of the French King on Flanders and Aquitaine, both fiefs of the French crown, the first having a close commercial relation with England, the second having both commercial and *feudal* relations. The wars of Edward I, especially the war against Wales, were successful. His work, however, proceeded during a crisis period in the development of Christendom—the first episodes in the long story of its disintegration into its constituent territorial units. The attempted unification of Britain under the English crown was an obvious response to the threat of French hegemony in Western Europe, as well as an enterprise in which both the royal family and a powerful section of the magnates could maintain and expand their existing territorial rights. Although aggression in Wales paid for itself as the Welsh borders became peaceful and prosperous, a source of wealth and manpower, aggression in Scotland intensified the evil which Edward meant to check: impoverishing border warfare which fostered local lawlessness; hostile feudatories in Scotland prepared to ally with the king's enemies, at home or overseas. But these results became obvious only after the death of Edward (1307).

Meanwhile, legal reforms were proceeding along lines foreshadowed in the reign of Henry III. The personal qualities of Edward, the qualities of a great general and administrator, were well adapted to the opportunities afforded by the situation. Now was the time when a war-loving king could control the leading groups within the realm: the baronage, the shire gentry, the clergy, the merchants, the justices and other officials. For the baronage, the group that had challenged his father and grandfather, had few members with considerable power. Baronies and earldoms had been divided or had lapsed. By adroit use of his feudal superiority, Edward was able to accumulate fresh demesne lands. The rank and file of the "barons" with whom Edward had to deal, were only little barons, whom he could summon to his council, or not, as seemed expedient to him. They could assist, but not capture or even challenge, his permanent advisory Council, now filled mainly with able officials. This Council, in which the King was predominant, did not only advise on high politics; it directed with minute business-like efficiency the various departments of state: the exchequer, the chancery, the law courts, the embryonic war department. Through them it controlled the local communities of the realm—the shires and boroughs. To important sessions of the Council, in which it dealt with the petitions of the realm and consulted the chief officials, (when, to use the current term, it was a parliament,) barons and bishops were often summoned. It became too a regular practice to summon representatives of the shires and some of the boroughs to such sessions. They came armed with powers from their communities to do whatever the king should require of them. Very often this was to consent to the levy of a subsidy. (Not until the reign of Edward III was their consent to a grant of customs necessary.) Possibly they sometimes assisted with legal business. Possibly they were useful agents for publicising the king's will in the shire courts on their return. But these gentry and burghers of the communities, the Commons, as they came to be called, were not yet a *House* of Commons: their presence was not essential to the holding of a parliament, as parliaments were then thought of. The Commons had nothing to do with the legislative work of Edward I's government. The Parliament which was to become the political instrument of the absolutist Tudor monarchy, and then of the rising bourgeoisie, was derived from the parliaments of Edward I, as this institution had its roots in the more casual parliaments of the later part of the reign of Henry III. On the whole however its forms and precedents were built up during the period of declining feudalism, when king and barons were often at loggerheads, and when the gentry were beginning to realize that they had a class interest separate from that of the feudalists. At this period of declining feudalism we must briefly glance.

CHAPTER VIII

THE BEGINNINGS OF THE DECLINE OF FEUDALISM

THE last phase of feudalism covers a long period of time: from the early decades of the fourteenth century to the revolution of the seventeenth century. The period was full of incident and variety; much has been written about it, many detailed problems have still to be worked out. In a sense it is the epilogue to the long story of feudal achievement which we have attempted to outline in preceding chapters. It is more significant however as a period of transition to an entirely new epoch of historical development. All that we shall suggest, in the brief remarks that follow, is that the first stage of this transition was largely conditioned by the tensions and conflicts which had developed in society during the preceding age of feudal progress; there was much disintegration and readjustment, but no feudal institutions were 'abolished'.

Feudal society in the age of Edward I, from top to bottom of its structure, was tense with the possibility of crisis. Kings and great landlords had increased their revenues and made the state more efficient only by intensifying the oppressive character of serfdom and kingly rule. They had built up an impressive body of law, the common law of the realm and the canon law of the Church; but, unless this law could be progressively modified, it would act as a drag on the further development of rural and urban life. We can regard the castles and cathedrals, the monasteries and walled cities of thirteenth century England as symbols of the self-confidence and European outlook of its kings and greater landlords, their ability to use the services of the communities subject to them. But how long could they continue to control and direct the development of feudal society as a whole in their own interests? Day-to-day manorial life on the great estates showed that there was some resistance to serfdom; it did not become easier by efficient supervision to prevent reeves and bailiffs from cheating. In spite of the economic, social and political predominance of the great landlords, the events of 1258-1267 and some passages in the reign of Edward I, had foreshadowed a time when the gentry and merchants would play a more independent part in politics than they had hitherto done. Would the crown, which had become so powerful in the reign of Edward I, collaborate with them consistently, and pursue at home and abroad a policy in conformity with their interests? Or would it attempt to rest exclusively on the support of the magnates? or would it try to maintain a precarious balance? There was the danger that it would not be able to resist using its power to tax the whole nation through the levy of customs and subsidies in or outside Parliament, to lead large scale military expeditions against neighbouring dominions, as Edward I had done; a danger, because feudal war, even if successful, was a boomerang. Whichever side won, productive forces were wasted; in the fourteenth century it opened up, both to the nobility and to the merchants, opportunities of increasing their wealth by reactionary means, at the expense of the rest of society. These were problems which history resolved. In fact the crown pursued a policy of war with France, which obliged it, in return for subsidies, to permit greater powers to gentry and merchants in Parliament. Meanwhile war nourished not only a few merchant profiteers, but also an ambitious and factious high nobility, overmighty subjects, who dominated both Parliament and Council under the Lancastrian kings. These institutions became the scene of a futile conflict of interests until the consolidation of the Tudor absolutism.

The ineffectiveness of the Commons in the parliaments at the end of the fourteenth century and their dependence either on one or other of the great magnates or the king and the Council is very clearly diagnosed in a satiric report of a parliament held in 1399-1400, obviously written by a knight of the shire who had some experience of the futility of the debates of his fellow members. In this case the debate followed a royal demand for money.

"Some members sat there like a nought in arithmetic that marks a place but had no meaning in itself. Some had taken bribes so that the shire which they represented had no advantage from their presence. Some were tattlers, who went to the king and warned him against men who were really good friends of his . . . . Some stammered and mumbled and did not know what they meant to say. Some were paid dependents and were afraid to take any steps without their master's orders. . . . . And some dashed ahead so recklessly that, like a ship driven by the wind, they would have gone on the rocks, had not the lords warned the master (perhaps the Speaker) that they had better keep to subjects which were their own business and which they understood; then they lowered their sails and took a wiser course. Some had been got at beforehand by the council and knew well enough how things would have to end, or the assembly would be sorry for it. . . . Some were quite openly more concerned about the money the king owed them than the interests of the commons who paid their salaries, and these were promised their reward; if they would vote the taxes, their debts would be paid them.

And some were so afraid of the great men that they
forsook righteousness.*

The clear predominance of the king in Parliament
characteristic of the reign of Edward I was no longer possible. Nor was the future predominance of the Commons
over the Lords forseeable: the situation in the reign of
Charles I when a member of the Commons remarked that
his fellow members "could buy the upper house (His
Majesty only excepted) thrice over". Nevertheless, as the
above report indicates, Parliamentary procedure was
developing.

European events, during these generations of disintegration and readjustment, exercised a decreasing influence on
the development of English society. There is little reason
to invoke the French wars, Papal politics or Papal finance†
as the primary reason for the growth of "national feeling".
In any case such a phrase should be suspect. It is true
that it was largely the growing strength of the French
monarchy which made a struggle to maintain English
dominion over Gascony inevitable. It seems to be true that
this war sometimes disturbed normal commercial intercourse between England and Flanders and in the end, led
to the loss of Gascony and the Gascon trade. War finance,
as we have suggested, was an influence in the development
of the House of Commons and the English merchant class,
and influenced many aspects of home politics. The plunder
and ransoms from successful campaigns was a means by
which the high nobility filled the gap between falling
incomes and rising costs and standards of living. The use
of the longbow, and finally, of artillery, in the war, decreased
the military importance of cavalry and castles. Nevertheless

* H. Cam, *Liberties and Communities,* pp. 230-231.

† While the Popes resided at Avignon, near the French frontier, 1305-
1378, they perfected their system of financial exactions from local
churches, and there was a strong French element in the College of
Cardinals. This "Babylonian Captivity" was followed by the Great
Schism, 1378-1414.

it is obvious that the character and prolongation of the war and the influence which it exerted on English life, was *primarily* an outcome of the changing social situation within England. Similarly if an explanation is sought for the spread of literacy among the laity, the development of English literature and of insular self-conscious trends in English political and ecclesiastical life, primary stress must be placed upon economic and social changes within England. The failure of the feudal nobility to consolidate their victories in France, after 1360, and again after 1422, was as much a reflection of the lines along which English society was developing as a consequence of French resistance. The tendency towards insularity was not peculiar; in Europe as a whole the decline of feudalism was bound up with the consolidation of compact territorial states which formed a framework within which a compromise between seignorial, ecclesiastical and bourgeois interests could be achieved.

Provisionally then, we can regard the complications of England's connections with Europe as of secondary importance. Let us look briefl· at the economic and social changes within England which took place while the weary Hundred Years War proceeded (1337-1453). The disintegration of the great estates as units of production and marketing, in a period of falling prices and disturbed and contracting overseas markets was clearly a very important process. For with this, in the long run, were closely connected the disintegration of the whole regime of manorial coercion, a decline in the total amount of wealth extracted from the peasantry, and the transfer to an upper statum of peasants and to the gentry, of the use of the former demesnes of great estates, and the virtual abandonment of forced labour in favour of wage labour. On the rich freeholders rested henceforward the onus of producing the marketable surplus of wool and foodstuffs. It is probable that, as this reorganisation was effected, and the middle of the fifteenth century is an approximate date for its completion, there was a decline in the amount of corn, and possibly of wool, produced for the market. Certainly the amount of wool and corn shipped overseas was greatly reduced, although an increasing quantity of wool was sold in the local markets to feed a growing native cloth industry. The export of undyed cloth was more important than the export of wool in the late fourteenth and fifteenth centuries.

What was the nature of the crisis which produced this readjustment? When the great landowners first reverted to the practice of renting or leasing, in small lots, some of their demesne and/or commuting some labour service for money rents, they did so, as we can surmise, because relatively high rents for acres of arable and pasture land could be exacted; the practice began towards the end of the boom period for wool and corn producers of which we have already written. From 1320 onwards, the prices obtainable for wool and foodstuffs began to fall. As there was not, so far as we know, any corresponding fall in rents, this was an added inducement for great landlords to become rentiers. For in view of the difficulties and overhead expenses of demesne farming, and the dead losses and debts which followed bad seasons, it is probable that a fall in prices would tip the balance in favour of a fixed cash revenue. After the outbreak of the French wars, an uncertain factor was introduced into overseas marketing; the general tendency for a "price scissors" to be formed, was emphasized.* In and after 1349 the decline of the peasant population, obviously resulting largely from the Black Death, which caused terrifying mortality in certain parts of England in 1349 and which thereafter recurred at intervals more sporadically, helped to create a severe shortage of labour. This interrupted, at least on some estates, the commutation of labour services for cash. Sooner or later it became impossible for bailiffs on the great estates to induce peasants to take up vacant holdings of land owing heavy servile works. There

* By a price scissors is meant here a fall in prices of goods produced by agriculture and a rise in prices of other commodities. See M. Dobb: *Studies in Development of Capitalism*, p. 58.

was a slackening in the demand for land, and the terms on which the great landlords leased their demesnes to tenants, of necessity became increasingly favourable to the latter. In other words, rents slumped. Instead of breaking up their demesnes into many small holdings, as they might have done if the boom conditions of 1300 had still been in existence, landlords were obliged to lease them in large blocks to prospering peasants and gentry of the neighbourhood, the relatively small circle of men who alone were able and willing to rent and farm more land, for the very moderate profits which were likely in the profound agricultural depression of the early fifteenth century.

At the height of the economic crisis, from 1349 to the peasants revolt of 1381 and the years following, there was a considerable amount of peasant agitation. This was partly directed against the Statute of Labourers of 1349, an attempt to peg down wages and prices to the levels prevailing before the Black Death and to prevent the movement of peasants, willing to work for wages, from the villages where they had a settlement. It was also directed against the whole condition of serfdom, as the Revolt of 1381 showed. But the Great Revolt was more than a protest. The peasant leaders who organised the march on London and conducted the negotiations with the King had a programme of political as well as of social reform. They were filled with the vision of an England in which communities of free peasant proprietors shared the land with the friendly gentry. Even in 1381, however, the disintegration of the village communities tended to make the fulfilment of this vision improbable. Even if the serfs had been formally emancipated in 1381 there is no doubt that the extension of peasant and gentry farms would have been accompanied by the further impoverishment of the majority of the peasantry. We have seen the beginnings of this two-fold tendency before 1300. Long before the enclosures of the sixteenth century, made at the expense of the lesser peasantry, raised a storm of social protest, the nascent squirarchy of declining feudalism had been consolidating their holdings in the open fields, buying up land, and making small enclosures of waste land, while the area of the holdings of the lesser peasantry, on the whole, dwindled.

The growth of regional markets in England for rural produce at the expense of the overseas trade, and the rise of a cloth export trade, were as we have suggested, the complementary processes to the gradual disintegration of large scale demesne farming and marketing. The native merchant class became more wealthy and secure and numerous, without making any essential changes in the mode of production. Their wealth was derived from urban or rural rents; from the profits of selling the work of urban craftsmen, organised in guilds which they controlled or of peasant spinners, weavers and fullers, living in the villages, to whom they gave piece work. Many merchants made profits out of the French wars; for contracts to provision, equip and transport armies to France went to merchants and from the outbreak of the Hundred Years war the crown mainly depended on native merchants for loans of money. If and when he had made a fortune, a merchant would buy land, endow charities, and became a pillar of feudal society. Neither consciously or unconsciously were the merchants acting as a revolutionary, anti-feudal force. The revolutionary history of the bourgeoisie begins only in the sixteenth century.

The expansion of exchange was however modifying political feudalism. *Feudal* tenures were no more abolished than serfdom, but it became increasingly inexpedient and unnecessary to exact personal services from fee-holders of any rank. Such incidents of feudal tenures were, by the fourteenth century, normally rent charges. Military services were normally secured by cash payments. Every great man surrounded himself with a circle of hired military retainers, salaried domestic servants, pensioners. The contract which bound a retainer to his master or pensioner to his patron was not a hereditary one; it was considerably less stable than the contract made in return for the hereditary fee of land. Inevitably the newer system fostered corruption in public life, both in the shires and at Westminster. The great landlords who moved within the court circle could put money in their pockets by securing military commands and offices in the state departments; services could be rewarded by pensions. Hence the struggle for influence at court between rival feudal groupings, which reached its climax in the so-called Wars of the Roses. Consequently, so far as the influence of the great landlords in politics was concerned, the period of the Hundred Years War saw an increase not a decline. What disappeared was the progressive legalistic reformism of the thirteenth century. Its place was taken by a cynical and reactionary attempt to pervert the law and the various institutions of central and local government, including Parliament, to sectional interests.

There was an economic basis to the scandals in the Church which the preachers of the time so constantly and hopelessly denounced. The Church had great landed wealth, but the income of most established churches was declining and the diminution in the regular incomes of the big lay feudalists dried up their patronage and made some of them quick to take up the cry of disendowment, first seriously raised in England by Wycliff. Into the complexities of this subject we will not go. An epilogue cannot be stretched to include an account of the background of the Reformation. Two points however about the changing rôle of the Church in the decline of feudalism may throw into relief the achievements of the church in the ages of feudal progress. First, piety often took the form of endowing schools, colleges at Oxford and Cambridge, hospitals and almshouses. These establishments, although controlled by the clergy, served the laity to a very large extent. Learning was ceasing to be a monopoly of the Church as sons of gentry and merchants passed from school to University or to the Inns of Court, for the legal profession became a very common means of entering public life. Second, in the greater towns, the craft guilds had acquired some of the features of religious fraternities: on a popular feast day, the feast of Corpus Christi for example, the crafts performed a cycle of religious plays in the streets of the town. These plays are only one example of ways in which religion was at last becoming popular, a medium in which, among many other things, social criticism could be conveyed. A better example, possibly, would be a religious poem like Langland's *Piers Plowman,* in which the invective, satire and exhortations of sermons preached by generations of friars and parish priests, were moulded into a poem written in English, in a style derived from old English heroic poetry, a poem eloquent of the grievances and fears and hopes of the lesser people of feudal society, the richer peasants, artisans, impoverished chantry priests and their like. Learning was reaching the laity; the popular culture which was developing so fast in villages and towns was a specifically Christian culture —but a Christian culture of many strands, containing within itself the seeds of Protestant heresies as well as orthodox Catholicism. Its medium was the English language, which for many purposes was taking the place of both Latin and French. It was the language of peasants, merchants and gentry; it could be used for a new popular literature and drama, for translating and adapting both the French literature of chivalry and for composing religious and legal treatises, for which Latin would earlier have been the normal medium of expression.

We have not attempted to describe the decline of feu dalism fully, even in the fourteenth and fifteenth centuries. Many aspects of it have not even been referred to. Perhaps however enough has been written to illustrate the point that on the whole the so-called decline of feudalism, even in its first stages, was not a period of retrogression, like the decline of the Roman Empire, but a period of readjustment. Some of the contradictions which had existed within society about 1300 began to resolve themselves; the middle classes were becoming influential, the great landlords began to lose their secure prodominance; but the institutional framework of feudalism was not destroyed. The way had been prepared for the Tudor absolutism, which in its turn produced conditions in which capitalism developed with some rapidity, more quickly indeed than in any other country of Europe. That this economic process was associated with so rich a growth of a national literature, music, religion, science, was largely due to the feudal heritage of the class who were rising to power. About 1500, both in town and country, the middle groups of feudal society were critical of, but soaked in, the material civilisation and ideology of feudalism. This for the time being was their strength.

A NOTE ON BOOKS

Secondary authorities only, dealing with books on the origins and development of English feudal society to the fourteenth century, are mentioned.

Reading should start, I think, from a basis of historical geography. Here two books are essential: C. Fox, *The Personality of Britain; its influence on inhabitants and invader in prehistoric and early historic times* (Cardiff, 1932); H. C. Darby, *Historical geography of England before 1800* (Cambridge, 1936). The latter volume contains useful working maps.

For pre-feudal history see: R. H. Hodgkin. *A History of the Anglo-Saxons,* 2 vols. (Oxford, 1935, useful for its many maps and illustrations); R. G. Collingwood and J. N. L. Myres, *Roman Britain and the English Settlements* (Oxford, 1937); H. M. Chadwick, *The Heroic Age.* (Cambridge, 1912).

J. R. Green's *Making of England* and *Conquest of England* (London, 1881, 1883) and W. Stubbs, *The Constitutional History of England,* 3 vols. (Oxford, 1773-8) and *Select Charters* (1st edition, Oxford, 1870, 9th revised edition by H. W. C. Davies, 1913) have influenced all subsequent study of English medieval history, to our own time. In order of their publication, these are some of the works which expand or revise Stubbs' work in important ways and/or show most clearly the results of study of new sources of evidence: J. H. Round, *Feudal England* (London, 1895); F. Pollock and F. W. Maitland, *History of English Law before Edward I,* 2 vols. (Cambridge, 1898); T. F. Tout, *Chapters in the Administrative History of England* (Manchester, 1920 *seq.*); H. Cam, *The Hundred and the Hundred Rolls* (London, 1930); F. M. Stenton, *First Century of English Feudalism* (Oxford, 1932); J. E. A. Jolliffe, *Prefeudal England; the*

Jutes (Oxford, 1933); and *Constitutional History of England* (London, 1937); N. Denholm-Young, *Seignorial Administration in England* (Oxford, 1937); F. M. Stenton, *Anglo-Saxon England* (Oxford, 1943); A. Lane-Poole, *Obligations of Society in the XII and XIII Centuries* (Oxford, 1944); F. M. Powicke, *Henry III and the Lord Edward,* 2 vols. (Oxford, 1947). Stubbs' work was characterised by the tacit assumption that law, administration and political institutions, local and central, lay and ecclesiastical, can best be studied apart from their economic environment; this assumption has not yet been discarded although in some of the later work mentioned above, economic matters are occasionally referred to. Jolliffe so far departed from the Stubbsian tradition that he excluded from his constitutional history, the development of ecclesiastical law and institution. The importance of the Lectures by F. M. Powicke on *Stephen Langton* (Oxford, 1928), lies, among other things, in his recognition of this interconnection. Important monographs on ecclesiastical history include: F. W. Maitland, *Roman Canon Law in the Church of England* (Cambridge, 1898); Z. N. Brooke, *English Church and the Papacy* (Cambridge, 1931); D. Knowles, *The Monastic Order in England* (Cambridge, 1941) and *The Religious Orders in England* (Cambridge, 1948). There is a useful short text book on general ecclesiastical history by M. Deanesley, *A History of the Medieval Church 590-1500* (London, 1925); H. Rashdall, *Universities of Europe in the Middle Ages,* in the revised edition (Oxford, 1936), is also relevant to an elementary study of English history, especially the section on the University of Oxford.

For the study of English peasant society and manorial organisation, the more useful of the pioneer works seem to me to be: F. Seebohm, *The English Village Community* (4th edition, London, 1890); F. W. Maitland, *Domesday Book and Beyond* (Cambridge, 1897) and P. Vinogradoff; *The Growth of the Manor* (London, 1904). Of more recent work, C. S. and C. S. Orwin, *The Open Fields* (Oxford, 1938) and

A NOTE ON BOOKS

G. C. Homans, *English Villagers in the Thirteenth Century* (1942). Important essays or lectures by M. Postan, E. A. Kosminsky and E. Power have been referred to in the footnotes to Chapter VI. Some of the results of the many regional studies, written since the time of Vinogradoff, are summarised in the contribution by N. Neilson to the *Cambridge Economic History*, Vol. I (Cambridge, 1941). This compilation of essays contains other material more indirectly relevant to the study of English agrarian history: for example, essays by R. Koebner and M. Bloch. The earlier works of W. J. Ashley, W. Cunningham and E. Lipson are still useful: for details see bibliography in the *Cambridge Economic History*.

Of short studies bearing on the subject matter of this little book, three are noteworthy: F. M. Powicke, *Medieval England* (Home University Library, 1930), (although the Anglo-Saxon period and peasant society are scarcely touched upon); chapters on English political-constitutional history, by various authors, in the *Cambridge Medieval History*, Vols. I-VII, to each of which are appended valuable bibliographies; G. O. Sayles, *Medieval Foundations of England* (London, 1948).

A NOTE ON ILLUSTRATIONS

THERE is an immense amount of original material which affords both evidence for the artistic and technical achievements of medieval society and illustrations of its everyday life and thought. This material is widely dispersed. It includes collections of antiquities housed in museums: in the Victoria and Albert Museum and the British Museum in London, for example, there are representative collections of coins, tools, weapons, armour, pottery, textiles, enamels, ivories, and many other works of art. The material also includes charters and other documents used in legal and administrative work, manuscript books, often illuminated, and the medieval "monuments" which still stand in many English villages and towns: sculptured crosses, castles, manor houses, churches. Some churches still retain their medieval glass windows, wall paintings, stone carving, bells, etc. The illustrations in this book do not therefore indicate the richness and variety of the available material.

INDEX

This is mainly concerned with subjects. Names of persons and places incidentally mentioned, do not appear.